ULTIMATE FORCE

ULTIMATE FORCE

AN EXPLOSIVE SAS TV DRAMA

DIANA HARRIS

B T BATSFORD • LONDON

To Andy, Gillian and Shelagh for the inspiration, and to Georgia, Ellie, Martha and Beth for distracting me with play-dough and piano practice.

A catalogue record for this book is available from the British Library.

ISBN 0 7134 8812 3

Printed in Spain by just Colour Graphic, S.L.

Designed by Zeta Jones

Volume © B T Batsford 2002

First published in 2002 by
B T Batsford
64 Brewery Road
London N7 9NT

A member of Chrysalis Books plc

CONTENTS

FOREWORD

When I told people of our plans to make an ITV series about the SAS, they were surprised because Bentley Productions has a reputation around the world for gentle drama, like *Midsomer Murders*. The truth is that I've always been a fan of action-adventure. We don't see enough of it because it is incredibly expensive to make.

Rob Heyland's scripts, written with the invaluable help of SAS hero Chris Ryan, open the door to an exciting and secretive world. The real SAS troopers are highly trained, incredibly focused men. They can speak three languages, operate complex machinery under fire, move inconspicuously from the jungle to the streets of Derry and kill terrorists in our name.

Our job was to bring that world to the screen, complete with bullets and pyrotechnics. Thanks to the hard work of a talented crew, three inspirational directors and an energetic group of actors who always went that extra mile, I believe *Ultimate Force* brings a new look to military drama, with an emphasis on hard-nosed reality.

Of course, it's not a documentary so some events that would take place over days or weeks are condensed into an hour or so. Henno Garvie played

by Ross Kemp gets shot twice but is back in time for the next episode. That's the way television works and I make no apology for it.

But within those limits of prime-time TV drama, time and money, we've done all we can to portray the SAS accurately and fairly. Bentley Productions is already developing another series – so read, watch and enjoy!

Brian True-May, 2002

The soldiers of Red Troop together at their base in Hereford.

INTRODUCTION

THE KILLING HOUSE

The action begins in a suburban house in semi-darkness. The sound of a TV game show filters through the gloom of the lounge. A young man lies on the settee, his body bound tightly with black masking tape, keen anticipation in his eyes. In front of him, his captors sit casually watching the television, the remains of an Indian takeaway scattered around. The hostage, Jamie, looks over to his friend, who is tied up beside him. Alex's eyes glance at the windows for any sign of movement amid the orange and brown flowery curtains. With a barely discernable shake of his head, Jamie nods towards the door instead.

Suddenly an explosion rips through the room, the door is blasted off its hinges, sparks fly, and a group of men clad in black overalls, balaclavas and respirators emerge through the smoke, their machine guns primed and ready. A split second later the lounge erupts to the sound of fierce gunfire as, one by one, the targets are shot at point blank range and eliminated. Jamie is struck on the face by flying blood but before he even knows if he's been hit, he is pulled from the building. With hearts pounding and eardrums all but shattered from the machine gun fire, he and Alex are left lying on the grass…

The smoke clears and a shadow passes over them. Jamie and Alex look up to see a dark figure, weapon across his chest, the blazing sun behind him. Pulling off the respirator to reveal his face, the man leans forward with a knife in his hand, picks off one of the lumps of red matter from Jamie's face and puts it in his mouth. 'I thought so. Watermelon. Nice touch', says the soldier, straight-faced.

This is Ricky Mann. Behind him appear Jem Poynton, Pete Twamley and Sam Leonard, followed closely by Sergeant Henno Garvie – a consummate soldier and leader of Red Troop. The dramatic hostage rescue is in fact an exercise in the 'Killing House' – an essential part of the initiation process for new recruits like Alex and Jamie to the Counter Revolutionary Warfare division of the SAS.

For those few minutes anyone watching would have believed they were witnessing a real SAS operation. Then the enemies are revealed as dummies with watermelons for heads. But while the rescue and shoot-out may be a dry run, the bullets are real. Every second counts and any hesitation could cost you your life. These are the skills practised relentlessly in the 'Killing House'. At any moment, Red Troop could be called upon to put their elite fighting skills to the test in a life or death operation.

So begins *Ultimate Force*, ITV1's multi-million pound prime-time film drama about the exploits of a crack SAS troop. And it starts as it means to go on. A no-holds-barred, exciting and explosive series about a regiment still shrouded in secrecy and mystique, a regiment that bears the motto 'Who Dares Wins'. Starring Ross Kemp as the tough and charismatic Sergeant Henno Garvie, the series is co-devised by former SAS soldier Chris Ryan, a member of the Bravo Two Zero patrol who survived against incredible odds behind enemy lines in Iraq during the Gulf War. Chris got together with acclaimed TV scriptwriter Rob Heyland, whose credits include *Without Motive*, *Bomber* and *Have Your Cake And Eat It*, to create *Ultimate Force* for Bentley Productions. The result is a unique insight into the real life workings of the SAS, combining rip-roaring action with a team of believable characters prepared to face life-threatening situations in the name of their country every day.

Joining Ross in *Ultimate Force*'s Red Troop are Jamie Draven and Sendhil Ramamurthy as newcomers Jamie Dow and Alex Leonard, whose induction to the 22nd Regiment is anything but gentle. Tony Curran plays old hand Pete Twamley, Danny Sapani is gentle giant Ricky Mann, Elliot Cowan is ladies' man Jem Poynton and Anthony Howell plays Alex's brother-in-arms, Sam. Alex Reid provides a touch of glamour as Captain Caroline Walshe, an officer from the Intelligence Corps assigned to the regiment, Jamie Bamber plays Henno's inexperienced but likeable troop commander, Lieutenant Dotsy Doheny, and Miles Anderson is the regiment's commanding officer, Colonel Aidan Dempsey. As well as serving as the series consultant, Chris Ryan also turns his talents to acting in the role of SAS sergeant Johnny Bell, the leader of Blue Troop.

Unlike many of today's television series, the emphasis in *Ultimate Force* is on action, although the characters of Red Troop are revealed in the course of their missions. Stopping the release of a lethal anthrax mutation, infiltrating an anti-capitalist group set on assassination, and a life-or-death bank siege are among the tasks facing Henno and his men. Henno's

reputation is at stake when an operation goes wrong in the complex political jigsaw of Northern Ireland, there's tragedy on a combat survival weekend – and the team find their skills, stamina and close-knit bond pushed to the limit when they are sent to hunt out a suspected war criminal in Bosnia.

Well-crafted stories and strong, energetic performances from the cast are the backbone of any hit drama – but there is much, much more to creating a major new series like *Ultimate Force* for ITV. Behind-the-scenes is the story of an 80-strong, talented and experienced crew, working through five months in mud, water and raining bullets to bring the concept to the screen.

Finding locations without any help from the Ministry of Defence, who still refuse to comment on the SAS; training actors to behave and shoot weapons like elite Special Forces soldiers who are the envy of the world, and creating fictional injuries during gun battles – without causing any real ones – are just part of the process. Stunts, special effects, pyrotechnics, firearms, helicopters, tanks and military uniforms are some other essential tools of the trade. Then there's funding the budget – and cooking thousands of bacon butties to keep everybody going…

Here is *Ultimate Force* – the official inside story.

IN THE BEGINNING

One of TV's most popular actors, a decorated SAS soldier turned best-selling author, and a production company renowned throughout the world sounds like a very good mix to create a hit drama. But even with the combination of Ross Kemp, Chris Ryan and Bentley Productions – the company behind the international hit *Midsomer Murders* – taking *Ultimate Force* from the page to the screen was not as straightforward as it might seem.

Like many programmes, its creation was organic. Characters and storylines grew from a melting pot of ideas and there was more than four years of discussion and the odd disappointment before the SAS drama reached fruition on ITV. Executive producer Brian True-May was at the heart of the process. According to him, 'action adventure series are great fun and very popular. We don't have enough of them, probably because they're too expensive to make. Since *The Professionals* there's not really been anything. ITV liked the idea of *Ultimate Force* but they didn't snap it up straight away. I couldn't for the life of me understand why.' Brian and the creative team refused to give in though – and the launch of the series on ITV1 is a tribute to their determination.

One of the people involved from the outset was Chris Ryan, a former SAS soldier whose amazing story of survival in the Gulf War was well documented in his best-selling book *The One That Got Away*. Chris has since become a successful novelist and his books were optioned by Chrysalis to be adapted for television.

Chris was introduced to TV scriptwriter Rob Heyland, who has penned a number of top-rating and acclaimed series, including *Between The Lines*, *Without Motive*, *Have Your Cake And Eat It* and *Bomber*. Explains Rob: '*The One That Got Away* was made for television, but Chris was not that happy with it. So when the idea of dramatizing his books was put to ITV, Nick Elliot, the head of drama at ITV Network Centre, suggested I might be the person to speak to. I went and met Mervyn Watson, who was then in charge of drama at Red Rooster, one of the Chrysalis companies, and looked at the stories. They are cracking reads but the opponents were primarily Russian or Arab which doesn't always work in TV drama, because, although it sounds harsh, the audience are not that interested in them.

'But the material about the SAS that the books contained, the world itself, was so amazing that I couldn't believe such a series had not been made. When you think that a new police series is commissioned almost every day of the week, virtually nothing has been done on the SAS. There aren't many things that are more British. The royal family, soldiers with big hairy hats on and cricket are all what some people call "Brand British". And one of the big things that would sell British as a brand is that we happen to have AMONG OUR ARMED FORCES THE UNDISPUTED ELITE KILLING MACHINE OF THE WORLD and yet we've not dramatized it in a TV series.'

Rob asked Chris to talk him through life in the SAS, starting right at the beginning – selection. Soldiers from other regiments can apply to try out for the 22nd Regiment, but the process of selection is tough beyond the comprehension of ordinary people. Challenging and exhausting, both physically and mentally, it takes six months of their lives – and only the cream of candidates ever make it through. 'I decided I wanted to do a pilot episode about selection', says Rob. 'The process is so mind-blowing, I thought let's see it in all its glory and use it as a way of introducing an audience to our characters. Two or three get through, and those are the guys we would go with for a series, plus the traditional tough sergeant from selection who ends up running their active service unit.

'It was a two-hour script, fantastically well contributed to by Chris and very rigorously researched. I sent it to ITV, and Nick Elliot and his deputy Jenny Reeks admired it. But they had one objection. They wanted it to be like the other action episodes that were going to follow. I didn't agree with them, but I respect them and knew I couldn't do anything about it. I'm conscious it's the way this business works.' By this time, the Chrysalis Television Group had amalgamated its drama output into Bentley Productions, headed by Brian True-May. Brian was surprised that his inherited project had hit a brick wall. 'The selection script was very good and there's nothing else on television like it. I went straight back to Nick and Jenny and asked them why on earth they had passed on it. After many more meetings, they finally came back and said OK.'

Bentley Productions' reputation as a preferred supplier of drama to ITV helped it win the commission for *Ultimate Force*. But ITV still wanted

Ultimate Force creator Rob Heyland has a cameo part – as a vicar.

changes made. They didn't want a pilot but a series. And they didn't want a film on selection, but an opening episode exploring what the SAS do best, with all guns blazing. For Rob and Chris this meant developing their characters a stage further. 'As a writer it wasn't too difficult because I already knew our two new recruits Jamie and Alex really well because they had been through selection', says Rob. 'Now we join them as they appear at Hereford and SAS headquarters at Stirling Lines, where they are allocated to Red Troop. The first episode is the real experience of coming in and being told "there's your chair, there's your bag and there's your gun – now what are we going to do today?" It's a bit like Club Med – shall we do parachuting, shoot at each other or drive cars? They're taken to the hangar and shown where their kit goes, then they're off to the Killing House and shot at for hours to get used to live firing.

'The script was meant to be an hour but I couldn't wedge it into one. As Nick and Jenny had just binned a two-hour episode I'd written, and so they didn't make me cry, they agreed to let this one run 90 minutes. We all called it a draw!' Rob then set to work with Chris on the remaining five episodes, using the selection pilot as background for one and drawing from the real experiences of SAS soldiers for others. 'We had already talked about some storylines and went to visit our mates at Hereford to pick up some more. Most of the episodes are fictionalized real events. There is no need to make up too much because these guys have done the most extraordinary things', he says.

'When I write any kind of drama I speak to people who are in the heart of that world and take out a little bit from each and put it together. More or less everything you see on screen has happened, although not necessarily in that scenario. Most we cannot identify, although elements of the bank robbery come from the Iranian Embassy siege, while others are from aircraft hijacks. The SAS is not absolutely air-tight but they are careful who they disseminate information to. Real SAS buffs will start piecing it together and people in the regiment will recognize things. To fit stories into an hour you have to bend things and compress the pace at which things happen, but I'm proud of what we've achieved. I think the SAS deserves an authentic evocation on screen.'

Getting the green light to go into production was just the beginning of the process for Brian True-May. His next big concern was paying for it. 'I knew immediately that the cost would be astronomic. ITV came up with a budget – a high amount – which was nowhere near enough. It costs far more than *Midsomer Murders*, but you can't make a series like this without spending money on guns, stunts and pyrotechnics.' To help fund the production, Bentley made use of the sale and leaseback scheme, a tax break that enabled investors to buy the rights to a production and then lease it back to the production company. Unfortunately, before *Ultimate Force* was complete, the TV part of the scheme was scrapped, cutting the level of available funding. 'We have made the series on a licence deal with ITV so I've had to borrow the money from Barclays Bank and don't get a penny until all the episodes are delivered. It's been a bit of a nightmare financially', says Brian. 'I'm terribly pleased with it, though. You have to be a bit brave in this business. In episode one where Red Troop storms the bank, the art department's budget went over by £100,000. It settled down but at the time I nearly fainted!'

The next task was casting a team of actors who could excel as credible members of the SAS. Securing former *EastEnder* Ross Kemp to play

Executive producer Brian True-May (left) and line producer Ian Strachan on location.

Sergeant Henno Garvie was a coup, although the character was developed after those of the new recruits Jamie Dow and Alex Leonard. Brian True-May explains: 'Originally it was going to be principally Jamie's story within an ensemble piece. But at an ITV drama party two years ago, director of programmes David Liddiment told me they had taken on Ross Kemp and asked me to think about a part for him. So we rewrote the episodes we had and put in this tough but fair leader of men. I believe Ross is perfect for the role of Henno. It suits him down to the ground.'

Rob Heyland wanted Red Troop to reflect the broad range of soldiers who are selected for service in the SAS. 'There's a real cultural mix. There are a lot of public school boys like me and Geordie boys like Chris Ryan. Guys from South Africa and a lot from the British Commonwealth. We haven't been able to get all of that across, but a lot of it is there.'

'For Jamie Dow I wanted to create someone who, if he didn't go into the army, would have ended up in prison. I wanted him to be damaged because I do think you're better off being damaged in the regiment. They don't want psychotics; they want intelligent people who can think calmly and clearly – but to get through six months of selection you have to have something strange to draw on. Usually that ability to be self-sufficient comes through being cut away from the normal comforts of

society, whether through abusive parents like Jamie or my own experience of boarding school and being sent away from your mother at the age of seven. Public school as preparation for the armed forces is just as valid a factor as the mean streets. Jamie and Alex reflect those opposite sides. They and Henno are deeply rooted within families that played a bigger part in earlier drafts of *Ultimate Force*. There's so little time to explore their home lives in an action piece, but it may come out in later series.'

The job of casting Jamie, Alex and the other members of Red Troop fell to *Ultimate Force* producer Peter Norris and Diarmuid Lawrence, who directed the first two episodes, along with casting director Jane Arnell. Jamie Draven, who starred in *Billy Elliot*, was first choice as Jamie Dow. Diarmuid Lawrence says: 'I worked with Jamie on *Messiah* and believe he's one of our coming stars. As well as Jamie, we were minded to cast people who replicate the real SAS – personalities who wouldn't be wonderful when bored.'

Casting Alex Leonard was less straightforward. 'There are two brothers in the regiment but one of them, Alex, is adopted and mixed race. Added to that, they come from a reasonably well-to-do background. We thought it was a nice concept, but didn't think we would be able to do it justice', says Peter Norris. 'Sendhil Ramamurthy was unavailable because of a feature film he was committed to do,

The troopers of Ultimate Force reflect the cultural mix of the real SAS.

but luckily for us the film was put back. When he walked through the door, we thought "that's it". He fitted all the criteria and he's a very good actor. His brother was easier because Sam is a well brought up military man and Anthony Howell is a good straight actor. In the opening scenes he looks so much part of the team that you couldn't guess what would happen to him.

'Jem Poynton fancies himself as a cool dude and he's always wearing shades. With no offence to Elliot Cowan, who got the job, we could have gone

The only woman in the 22nd Regiment – Captain Caroline Walshe.

for a really pretty boy, but we looked for someone with a personality and Elliot's got that in spades. He was an unknown face at the time and we felt he was a star in the making.'

Rob Heyland wrote a brief character breakdown for each role – but sometimes it wasn't possible to find an exact match, as Peter explains: 'You sometimes have to ignore elements of the biographies and go for the best actor, rather than somebody who absolutely fits the bill. Because **RED TROOP IS BASED ON PEOPLE CHRIS RYAN KNEW**, it's never a good idea for legal reasons to go strictly on what's written either. It's a blend – Chris describes a character, Rob transposes it on to a page, I cast someone and the actor gives an interpretation. You end up with a less factual person, but the mix still represents the diversity of people in the SAS.

'Originally the character of Ricky Mann was of Maori extraction. Apparently there are several Maoris in the SAS who joined from the New Zealand equivalent. We were restricted by the number of people who match that description, so rather than trying endlessly to fill a particular ethnic pigeonhole, we cast in the spirit of Ricky, who is a cook, larger-than-life, with a particular brand of humour. We ended up with Danny Sapani, who is a brilliant actor so I think it was the right thing to do. Similarly Pete Twamley was not written as Scots but we decided Tony Curran was best for the role. He came with a bit of received background because he's been cast in darker roles in the past, as a villainous, working-class Scot. But I knew he was more diverse than that, and he's come across on screen as being rough and tough, but sympathetic, too.'

A drama about the SAS is necessarily male dominated, but one female character has a very important role. Captain Caroline Walshe is an intelligence officer attached to the regiment. Although not technically an SAS officer, she is treated as a valued member of the team for the duration of her assignment. Says Peter Norris: 'Caroline was a difficult one. We wanted to pay more than lip service to the fact that she has an important role and not fall into the cliché of choosing a dolly-bird. Alex Reid is obviously a very good-looking actress but you also believe there is something going on behind the eyes – that she is determined and steely and would succeed in a man's world. Caroline wants to prove herself but Henno is protective of her and worries that if she becomes a victim it would upset the troops far more than if a male trooper was injured or killed. In the second episode we let Caroline get into the action and it ends with her sticking her finger up at the men. I think that sums her up. Also, Alex Reid more than held her own, filming with a group of lads. **SHE WAS ONE OF THE BOYS**.'

The other officers are the troop commander Dotsy Doheny and regiment commander Aidan Dempsey – roles that went to actors Jamie Bamber and Miles Anderson. 'There is quite a lot of ribaldry about Dotsy being an inexperienced 'Rupert' so you could play him as a one-dimensional cartoon character, but that would hardly be fair. Jamie

The officers – troop commander Dotsy Doheny, Captain Caroline Walshe and regiment commander Aidan Dempsey.

Bamber is Cambridge-educated but he is a very fit actor and comes across as a believable member of the team', says Peter. 'I think Dempsey is a really important character, too. I've read articles about David Stirling, who created the SAS, and like him, Miles has that ability to be aloof one moment and matey the next, with an infinite trust in his men. Miles is not obvious because he's from Zimbabwe, but I think he's one of the best pieces of casting we did. He might only have one scene in an episode, but if viewers don't believe the smaller characters, it affects the way they look at the whole series.'

Because *Ultimate Force* is an ensemble piece, it is

inevitable that some of the cast are given bigger slices of the action than others. Says executive producer Brian True-May: 'At the moment, Ross and Jamie get the lion's share of the action but we hope to develop the other characters as time goes on.'

As important as casting was the need to assemble a crew with the right talent and experience to make the series on schedule and within the budget. Peter Norris, who has worked on such diverse dramas as *Between The Lines*, *A Young Person's Guide to Becoming A Rockstar* and *My Uncle Silas*, saw *Ultimate Force* as an attempt to go back to old-fashioned television, with a self-contained story every week.

Determined the series would be as truthful as possible, he approached the Ministry of Defence. 'We told them what we were doing and they said they would offer us no co-operation at all. It's because they do not acknowledge the existence of Special Forces like the SAS. So, unlike series like *Red Cap* or *Soldier Soldier*, we don't have any help in terms of locations or facilities. That's the downside, but I'm not bemoaning the fact. In a way it's quite good because you don't want to feel you've got any form of sanction or that it has to be authorized.'

The involvement of Chris Ryan reassured Peter that he could make an accurate drama without the MOD's help. 'Chris gave the actors a lot of confidence and another thing he brought us is the regiment's camaraderie and gallows humour. When someone is injured or dies their attitude is not one that you would expect. They laugh and joke and say they didn't like the man anyway. They know death can be part of the job and don't allow themselves to mourn. There's an expression that's used in the first and last episode when anyone gets too sentimental about a colleague. Somebody interrupts and says "that's enough, we're not American" or "enough of the social". The trick is how much of that you believe. Of course these people care, but they are trained enough to know that if they did break down, it would open up a gulf in them and affect the way they work. That's really what the show is about. We like the SAS, their exploits are splattered in the tabloids – but do we really know what they go through in our name?'

The six episodes cover a wide range of operations, taking Red Troop on hostage rescues, undercover missions, surveillance tasks and anti-terrorist hits at home and abroad.

In the opening episode, entitled 'The Killing House', Red Troop is called to an armed robbery at a bank. Peter Norris explains: 'It's a gung-ho episode which comes soon after Jamie and Alex's initiation in the Killing House. The bank raid goes wrong and hostages are taken. The rule is that if there are shots fired in a hostage situation you can call in the SAS. Until then, it's a police operation. Once it becomes under military control, your expectations of the outcome should change. If you're expecting enemies coming out with their hands up, you've called in the wrong people. The Iranian Embassy siege was a similar sort of operation – people held hostage in a very secure building, shots being fired and the necessity to get in there and clean them out. My subtitle for *Ultimate Force* would be "no prisoners taken". There's a nice line in the first episode when the police ask if the SAS are going to go into the bank and shoot everyone. The SAS reply "it's a bit more sophisticated than that", but you know in a way it isn't. That's what you pay for when you call in the SAS.'

In Episode Two, 'Just A Target', the style changes as the story follows the work done by the SAS both in the UK and abroad on surveillance. 'The episode features a gun which almost becomes a character itself. It's not any old gun, it's a sniper's rifle, which can be fired from a mile away and take a whole wall out. It used to be a favourite of the IRA. Red Troop have to track and infiltrate an anti-globalization group who have access to the gun and who attempt to assassinate an international banker with it. We see the lads bugging a building in a race against time to find the weapon', explains Peter.

Episode Three, 'Natural Selection', covers the trials and tribulations of SAS selection. 'We meet a new character called Mick Sharp, played by Laurence Fox. He's full of malapropisms and is quite funny. However, he has failed selection once and is on his second and last attempt to do it', says Peter. 'The recruits have to go over fields, mountains and streams without being given any food, while trying to evade a group of Paratroopers called the Hunter Force who will attack them on sight. It's a highly dangerous game and added to that is the twist of someone who is bent on killing off some of the recruits. The episode shows what you have to go through on selection with a

The series see Red Troop on a wide range of operations, including undercover missions abroad.

murder mystery plot thrown in as well.'

Episode Four, 'Breakout', started off as a story about a plane hijacked on the ground. Peter made the decision to change the episode for practical reasons. 'I didn't think anyone would give us the facilities to do a plane hijack so we took the basic idea and put it into a chemical laboratory developing a strain of anthrax. A group of terrorists try to steal the anthrax, but get locked into the building with hostages and victims. Our guys have to get in there before the terrorists get out with the anthrax or by accident release it. It's a good action adventure episode showing the storming of a building, but during it our hero Henno Garvie gets shot twice and is seen lying in a pool of blood.'

The two final episodes are both set outside England. Episode five, entitled 'The Killing of a One-Eyed Bookie', is in Northern Ireland, while the final episode, 'Something To Do With Justice', sees Red Troop in action in Bosnia. 'The Northern Ireland episode is a fair reflection of the duties they perform', says Peter. 'There's a threat to the life of a putative loyalist politician and Jamie is doubling as a decoy. A bungled assassination attempt leads to Jamie being kidnapped by a republican splinter group. It's quite bloody and doesn't shy away from the fact that he would be tortured and killed. Henno takes it quite badly to lose a man. But within that comes the gallows humour again. When an SAS man dies, the others auction off his effects, mainly to give money to the relatives – but it seems fairly callous. So we show our troop wondering what size Jamie's boots are. Then, because of what happens in Northern Ireland, Henno and Pete Twamley are kicked out of the SAS at the beginning of episode six. They are recruited by mercenaries to train a militia force, led by a war criminal in Bosnia, while the real SAS guys are sent in to try and snatch him. It's a complicated setup but has a little dalliance for Henno with a Serbian doctor called Masha. In the last scene of the penultimate day of shooting, there was a scene where Henno is given an internal examination by this doctor as part of their security checks. Thankfully for Ross it was a closed set!'

Peter believes the episodes reflect the real range of SAS activities – in the regiment there's never a dull moment. 'SAS soldiers are very self-motivated. If they're not on operations, they dream up exercises or send them off on jungle treks or arctic expeditions or to train other troops. These are not the sort of men to sit around playing cards and the one thing you won't see them doing is parading up and down. They're too highly trained and too dangerous a force to be left idling at home.' And, luckily for fans of *Ultimate Force*, stories about Red Troop and the elite band of soldiers who are the inspiration for them show no sign of running out. Says Rob Heyland: 'There are new things happening involving the SAS in Sierra Leone and Afghanistan and South America, but also in the British Isles. The guys are out there and they're as busy as they ever were.'

CHRIS RYAN
AND THE REAL SAS

For any television series based around a profession or specific walk of life, the role of the consultant is a valuable one. Without the services of an adviser who knows the programme's world from top to bottom, small but significant details could easily be overlooked. For a series on the Special Air Service, one of the world's premier Special Forces units, having inside knowledge is not just valuable but vital, especially as the Ministry of Defence refused to play any part. Without the involvement of former SAS soldier Chris Ryan, *Ultimate Force* would not have been made.

Since its formation as a desert raiding force during World War II, the 22nd SAS has been renowned for the secrecy of its methods and operations. Although the regiment saw action behind enemy lines in Africa and Europe, and was deployed after the war in Malaya, Borneo, Aden, Oman and Northern Ireland, many people were simply not aware of its existence. It was when the SAS staged a successful assault on the Iranian Embassy in London in 1980 after terrorists seized the building, taking 26 hostages, that their actions made news headlines around the world. Thanks to their courageous, fast and effective counter-terrorist activity at the siege, and during the Mogadishu aircraft hijack three years earlier, the troopers' reputation as outstanding professional warriors was secured. Interest in the regiment surged, but the gates to its headquarters in Hereford remained closely guarded. **AS FEW AS 200 SOLDIERS ARE CHOSEN FOR SERVICE AT ANY ONE TIME,** and the selection process is regarded as one of the toughest of its kind. Individuals who do make it through are rewarded with a beige beret bearing the famed winged dagger and the honour of belonging to an elite fighting force.

The SAS remains a clandestine organization, despite the great interest in its activities. Troopers' names are kept secret and operations in the Gulf and Falklands wars have only become known over time. The policy on keeping quiet – in relation to recent SAS missions in such countries as Sierra Leone and Afghanistan – continues. Creating a brand new ITV series about the SAS and a crack troop serving within the Counter Revolutionary Warfare division required a great deal of specialist knowledge. Fortunately this was information and advice that Chris Ryan, a decorated former trooper and co-deviser of the drama, was perfectly placed to provide. As well as consultant, Chris Ryan also plays the part of SAS sergeant Johnny Bell.

Chris was born in 1961 in a village near Newcastle. At the age of 16 he attached himself unofficially to 'C' Squadron of 23rd Special Air Service, the territorial regiment based at Prudhoe in Northumberland. Over the next seven years he covered hundreds of miles of moor and mountain on training exercises. In 1984, he joined 22nd SAS and completed three tours of duty, which took him to many parts of the world. He also worked extensively in the counter-terrorism field, serving as an assaulter, sniper and finally Sniper Team Commander on the SP or Special Projects team.

Chris is best known, though, as one of the surviving members of the Bravo Two Zero patrol, an eight man team dropped deep behind Iraqi lines during the Gulf War to search for mobile Scud missile launchers. After the team was compromised, the troopers tried to escape but became split up. Three men were killed and four were captured. Chris alone managed to make it across the Syrian border to safety – a journey of 180 miles, on foot, through enemy fire and bad weather.

For his escape from Iraq in January 1991, he was awarded the Military Medal. Chris left the SAS in 1994, and he has since combined security and public-speaking work with a successful writing career. Chris's incredible achievements in the Gulf were documented in his first book, *The One That Got Away*, which became a number-one bestseller. He has since written six bestselling novels and his most recent book, *Land of Fire*, was published this summer. He is also the author of *Chris Ryan's SAS*

Chris Ryan (left) passed on invaluable tips about SAS life to Ross Kemp.

Fitness Book and two adventure stories for children featuring basic survival tips.

Chris began his involvement with *Ultimate Force* when Chrysalis TV company Red Rooster approached him with the idea of putting his novels on screen. He was introduced to scriptwriter Rob Heyland and the series was born. Says Chris: 'We decided to do a brand-new series rather than adapting the novels. I would come up with situations and scenarios that I was either involved in or had heard about and Rob put them into a script format. I described different guys I knew in the regiment and how situations would develop, and we crammed that into the 60 minutes.

'We tried to include a broad range of personalities. Henno is a bit more serious than the others, because he's carrying a lot of weight on his shoulders. He's very typical of a guy in his later years in the regiment. Danny is very quiet, but a solid personality; Twamley is quite middle of the road, and Jamie is typical of a newcomer. He watches the others, sucks in all the information and gradually gets more involved. His progress really covers a year or so, but in *Ultimate Force* it has to be done in weeks, of course.'

Once the characters of Red Troop had been cast, Chris took the new 'recruits' on a survival-training weekend. He explains: 'Originally it was supposed to be a week in the Brecon Beacons where we hold SAS selection, but because of foot and mouth it got cancelled. Without taking anything away from the cast, it would probably have been a bit too demanding for them. Then I suggested taking them

on the Black Mountains but we couldn't get insurance cover for them there. So we ended up in the Chilterns for a weekend. I took a friend and we walked around and told stories, which I guess was helpful because it developed their characters and perception of what an SAS soldier was like. We did a bit of running and I kept them out overnight. We slept under ponchos – a canvas cover made from nylon sheeting – which was a bit uncomfortable.'

After their sleep among the elements, Ross Kemp and the other actors tried their hand at using weapons before being taken through the basic attack plan for storming a building. 'I wanted to give them some idea of where they would stand, how they would hold the weapon and move with it. **IF SOMEBODY HASN'T BEEN TRAINED WITH A WEAPON THEY'LL STAND OUT A MILE.** But if you get someone with a bit of training, again that stands out and looks very professional. The gun moves as part of the body. Every single one of them enjoyed it. We got the pistols out and we got to fire live rounds, which is very difficult to do in this country because you need a special licence. Then they got to fire the MP5, which is a machine gun. There were smiles all round.'

Training done, it was time to start filming. Again Chris was on hand to advise and ensure the drama remained authentic. 'Whenever there was an action scene I tried to be there. My name's attached to the series and I want it to look right. I want the regiment to be portrayed in a good light as professional soldiers. We've all got chinks in our

Chris, Jamie Draven and Sendhil Ramamurthy relax between takes at the storming of the bank (episode 1).

armour but once the work starts, the lads become very serious. I hope that comes across. When you see it on screen, some of the scenes are very lifelike. In the bank siege, the sounds and the movement are very quick and unemotional. Everything is happening very fast and you get the sense of confusion. It's probably the closest you could get without actually being in a situation like that. The selection episode rings true, too; the guys are dressed just as we were in World War II uniforms, although no-one was coming across and actually killing us when I did it. There is something on all the episodes that brought back memories. Getting that kit on again and firing the weapons sparked things back.'

Adds Chris: 'I think it is a hard-hitting series. Some people might not realise that when the regiment is sent into a situation, it is sent to resolve it with violence. You've got the police to go and arrest people and you've got negotiators to talk people out. But when a Minister signs it over to the military it's likely there will be casualties.'

Some of those casualties could end up being the troopers themselves, which Chris knows only too well. During his 10 years' service, he attended 18 SAS funerals. He was also shot at, suffered a fractured skull and a compound fracture in his ankle. 'I wanted *Ultimate Force* to show how things go wrong as well as right, even with a lot of planning. That's the job. You know you're dealing with slim odds. If you turned up to an office and 18 people died through work-related injuries, most people would get out.'

Burying a friend and colleague is a tragic but inevitable part of SAS life. In his 10 years' service, Chris attended 18 such funerals.

Black humour is the SAS way of coping with the appalling toll of death and injury. 'When it's not serious, the guys want to be laughing. It's how they survive. The one who was killed wouldn't want anyone sitting there moping and crying. You just go out for a drink, get it out of your system that night and then go to work the next day. We'd also have auctions to sell off a guy's equipment.

'The humour is often very childish as well. We had a cannon ball in B Squadron. This thing weighed about 30 pounds but it used to follow us all over the world, even to the Gulf. Someone would find it in his pack after walking for eight hours. There'd be curses and everyone would be laughing. Right from the desert to the jungle someone would end up with it. It was a way of keeping one another going. It's the humour of *Ultimate Force* that the real guys like best. In episode two, when the MI5 officer has to climb out of the window to escape being seen, he panics and says "I can't jump". Twamley just pulls his arms away and he falls down. That's the type of thing I would like to see more of. I'd also like to do an episode set in the desert and I think it would be good to get into the families a bit more. When Jamie goes back to see his mother in episode one it is emotional and moving. **GOOD DRAMA TAKES YOU ON A ROLLER-COASTER RIDE.** One minute, something's tugging on your heartstrings, the next minute you're laughing, then you're having a fright because there's rounds going down.'

There are a couple of scenes, however, where Chris had to accept the use of dramatic licence.

'Some of the scenes were quite hard to go along with but in the long run I realised they were a way of describing a situation better for television. For example, in episode one, when Red Troop is in the hotel cooking a candlelit dinner, it's not as glamorous as that. In real life you're lying in camp beds with a mobile kitchen nearby. I didn't really approve of them drinking alcohol on the night before a mission either, because the SAS soldiers are very professional once work begins. But I suppose that scene shows how they look after each other, like a big band of brothers. It also shows that Henno knows his wine and can speak fluent French. The regiment is very good at languages."

Working on the series may have brought back memories, but Chris has no regrets about leaving the SAS. 'It was the best 10 years of my life but when I'd made the decision I couldn't turn back or ponder on it. I had to leave and that was it. I do miss it and I keep in touch with friends, but I suppose if I was honest and ran through the scenarios they have to do, I probably wouldn't be too happy doing them any more. The last job in Sierra Leone sounded quite frightening and the battle in Afghanistan was horrendous. It is a young man's job, especially when the enemy is only about 20 feet away and they're still coming at you. That's not for me any more. They do a good job but it really catches up with you. It's not conducive to looking good!

'For a lot of lads it's difficult to leave because in the army generally you're looked after very well. Your pay goes in and there's no real chance of being made redundant. There's a dentist and doctor on camp, your meals are prepared and there's a house if you want one. Then all of a sudden you're out in the big bad world and you've got to get a job. It's harder outside than it is inside. When I got out I was working with a bodyguard team along with a bunch of other ex-regiment guys so it was home from home really. I'd also worked as a civilian before I joined the army.'

Chris was very impressed with the actors who stepped into his shoes in *Ultimate Force*. 'They got really into it and started to get a bit huffy when the stunt men came in to take over on various scenes. It was good to see how keen they were to take part in the action.' Whether they would make the grade as a real trooper is another question, though. 'It's not fair to judge because an SAS soldier has been in the army for some time and spends six months on selection. I've seen it from both sides of the fence – I've passed selection and my last two years were spent selecting and training guys. They're constantly on operations and are under a lot of pressure. One mate of mine only spent two weeks in his own home last year. Possibly, if you put those actors on selection, one or two might pass, but I think they do their job very well on screen – which is why you don't have SAS guys winning Oscars.'

The boot was on the other foot when tough guy Chris played the part of Johnny Bell in *Ultimate*

Putting on the SAS "blacks" and firing weapons brought back mixed memories for Chris.

Force. 'I've been in some frightening situations in my life, but I've never been so frightened in all my life as when I was acting. My first scene with Ross Kemp went OK from my point of view and I wasn't even aware of the 30 people standing behind the camera, but on episode six for some reason I just flipped. My nervousness must have come out because the director told me to take a couple of deep breaths and calm down. For some reason I couldn't control the panic and the fear was phenomenal. You can know your lines and what's going to happen but as soon as they say "action" for some reason the old adrenaline gets pumped through the body, your voice gets very nervous, all your lines gel together and everything goes black. God knows what it must be like to be on stage in front of a live audience doing Shakespeare. I know it seems back to front for me to be so terrified of it. But I also get very nervous when I'm interviewed in crowds, like at a book signing. **LOOKING AT THAT CAMERA AND THINKING OF ALL THE PEOPLE WATCHING ME CAN BE FRIGHTENING.** With the SAS you develop an ability to disappear within crowds. We could be in control of a situation without anyone even knowing we were there, so it's the opposite of what I'm used to.

'I must say it's given me an admiration for the acting profession. When I sit and watch TV now, I forget the storyline and start looking at how the people are acting and holding themselves. You can say something without opening your mouth using body language and facial movements. If I do get the

Make-up designer Vanessa Johnson applies finishing touches to Chris before the cameras roll.

Left: *Red Troop*

chance to do it again I'd like to do one of those clinics or courses for TV. It's a three-dimensional skill and there's so much to do. Actors have trained and trained, then there's me worrying over five words. It was a challenge for me to conquer that fear.'

Despite Chris's fears, *Ultimate Force* director Tim Leandro describes him as a 'cracking actor'. And producer Peter Norris recognizes the difference that Chris's contribution has made. 'The SAS is one of those regiments about which there's an awful lot of mystique. No-one's going to tell you if you got it right but it doesn't half make you feel good as a producer to know that you've got someone who's been right in the thick of things. Chris helped us with all the technicalities to make it as near accurate as possible. The SAS are self-disciplined and self-motivated but they are also one of the most individualistic of regiments. Because they've gone through such an arduous process to get in, they're allowed some latitude within the regiment. Yes, you have to be at the peak of your profession, but you can be an individual as well. Chris being there has rubbed off on the actors, giving them the confidence to be their own characters – and that comes across on screen.'

Tough guy Chris admits he had to conquer a fear of acting to appear in Ultimate Force.

CREATING THE SAS ON TELEVISION

The former US army base at Upper Heyford is the perfect atmospheric setting for SAS HQ Stirling Lines.

Creating a series about the SAS without any official help from the real-life army was just one of the challenges facing the crew assembled to work on *Ultimate Force*.

For Peter Norris and his team, the tasks included finding a believable headquarters for Red Troop, obtaining hardware such as tanks and helicopters, designing military props and uniforms and teaching the actors to behave like real soldiers. And before they were through, they would be asked to set episodes in the Welsh mountains, a French chateau, Northern Ireland and Eire and even the valleys of Bosnia. To make matters worse, budgetary constraints meant all these locations had to be within easy travelling distance of the M25!

Location manager Rupert Bray began work even ahead of the directors. Rupert was soon joined by production designer Gary Williamson, whose job it was to deliver the feel and concept required by the script. The pair of them set out to find where and how *Ultimate Force* could be filmed. Luckily, Rupert brought some expert knowledge of his own – he served with the Parachute Regiment for a year before joining the Scots Guards as a captain for six years. 'I always knew that finding a barracks home for Red Troop would be difficult. I was determined to make it look authentic and it was a real help having a military background – but at some stages I was overwhelmed with everything we had to do.'

For the SAS base, Rupert persuaded production bosses to break one of their rules – that all locations had to be within 35 miles of Bentley Productions' base at Pinewood Studios. 'I visited the former US base at Upper Heyford and it was perfect. The hangars provide a regimental feel on a vast scale. There is high security fencing, hardened concrete shelters and barrack blocks. It would have been almost impossible and prohibitively expensive to build anything like it. But it was 50 miles away. I thought it was worth it and luckily everyone agreed.' Upper Heyford in Oxfordshire is the site of a former Air Force base that was used by the Americans under British control. After reassuring management about the way it would be featured, the base was transformed into Stirling Lines, the home of Red Troop. A strong image for the series, the location is also used for the opening credits of the series. Gary Williamson says: 'Upper Heyford is desolate and the hangars against the flat skyline was perfect for SAS territory. The location is so evocative and atmospheric. Everything we got was empty so we had to paint it and prop it – but it was a gift.'

The barracks was an important location but there were others to find. Gary and Rupert were continually challenged throughout the five-month shoot, as they worked closely with *Ultimate Force*'s three directors – Diarmuid Lawrence, Tom Clegg and Tim Leandro. Gary explains: 'My job is to talk to the director and find out what he has in his head for a particular scene, then go off with Rupert and trawl what's on offer. Then we go back to places with the director to find out what he really likes. *Ultimate Force* was location-led because we didn't have the money to build anything on the scale we needed. I always go for gold and hope it will work.'

Diarmuid Lawrence, whose previous credits include *Messiah*, Jane Austen's *Emma* and *Anglo Saxon Attitudes*, was director for the first two episodes. He came on board six weeks before filming began. 'I got involved very soon after the production was greenlit', says Diarmuid. 'It's very appealing to be

Director Diarmuid Lawrence (left) with Jamie Draven, an actor he describes as "one of our coming stars".

involved from the beginning. People have described the pre-production process as a Dutch auction. You start with the writer, producer and director's best ideas of how to do it, and then go through all the pragmatic processes of what can be afforded in terms of time and money. It's a case of trying to nail it before it's come down more than you can bear. You try to preserve as much of that first vision as you can. It sounds fairly negative, but the upside of that is being able to set a style.

'The style I was after is very camera-active and intimate. It's not a television show for careful, long, lyrical passes. We managed to pick a cameraman in Kevin Rowley who is very happy being physical, running the camera through the smoke and dust, although he got a few more bruises than he had anticipated. He is also the Director of Photography and combines his camerawork with lighting brilliantly.'

The series begins with a live firing exercise in the so-called Killing House. 'It was great to go straight

Firing live ammunition is a regular part of SAS work.

into the story and pick up the characters along the way. Episode one was a relatively easy ride for me, because the new boys are introduced to the old boys as they are introduced to the audience', says Diarmuid. 'Nothing quite concentrates the attention like firing live rounds in the Killing House.

'Jamie and Alex have to trust that no-one's going to put a shot through their heads in the dark. Then they ask to go back in and do the live firing themselves. There is reciprocal bonding going on and they have to trust each other completely.

'Afterwards the new boys have a chance to prove themselves in a real operation. You can't have endless gunfire because people get bored. What I like is the build up to the siege in the bank. After you've established the Killing House scene is an exercise, not a rescue, you then see a bunch of real bad guys. Everyone knows the bank robbers and the SAS are going to meet. It's simply a question of how and when, and what the outcome will be. It's a classic urban anti-terrorist assault and my job was building up the tension.'

Finding a house to blow up repeatedly and a bank that SAS troopers could storm was a job for Rupert Bray and Gary Williamson. **AN ALL-ACTION SAS DRAMA** with masses of smoke and explosions means it's often impossible to use someone's domestic house because of possible damage, so the scenario is recreated in a derelict building. According to Gary, 'the SAS can make a Killing House out of anything and if I'd been given the money I would have liked to do one out of old tyres. That way, the guy that's training the recruits can stand on scaffolding

Henno (right) and Dotsy make plans for the bank siege in episode 1: 'The Killing House'.

around the rooms and observe. But it's quite a costly thing to do. Instead we looked for an empty house. It was hard to find a location that was safe – most of them had rotten floors that you could never put a crew into. Rupert found the one we used on a hospital site near Gatwick. Next to it was a building still housing mentally-ill patients but they still let us let off explosions and guns.'

Peter Hallam is the property master responsible for dressing the scene once items have been sourced by prop buyer Cathy Cosgrove. He says: 'The Killing

House started out as a disused building full of damp and mould. It had to be gutted, painted, wallpapered, re-glazed, carpeted and furnished to give the required impression. That short interior sequence took four days to dress and two days to shoot. And, yes, those exploding watermelons were real, especially imported because they were out of season.'

The bank proved to be a tricky location for Rupert Bray. 'It was a good building but my worst location. It was on a fairly busy street in Hampton and we needed to close the road but the council said no. **SO WE HAD TO FILM DURING THE DAY, TRYING TO KEEP EVERYBODY HAPPY.** We only just got it by the skin of our teeth.' Explosions and stunts in such a built-up area required special care. 'We had to blow up the windows but we couldn't use real or toughened glass because it might have hit someone', explains Gary Williamson. 'Sugar glass is usually an option but you can't get it four foot square like we needed. Instead we came up with a brilliant idea – plastic dustsheets from B&Q, which we stretched over a frame! One of the guys puts a detonator on to the glass, then we cut the action, put our cling film windows in and the explosion goes off.'

From a bank siege, Gary and Rupert went straight to work on finding a French chateau and south London commune for episode two. The story follows the attempted assassination of a European

Plastic dustsheets doubled as glass in the bank siege to stop shards shattering over a busy London street.

banker with a highly dangerous and rare sniper's rifle, and the race to find the weapon among a group of anti-capitalists. 'The hit was written for a modern glass building but since September 11th corporate businesses don't really want to know film crews that blow things up. So we went for something traditional and ended up with a "chateau", which was really Waddesdon Manor near Aylesbury', says Gary. 'It came up trumps in the end because we were also able to use an old-fashioned lift there to depict another scene in Prague, where a character has his briefcase snatched.

'The protestors' squat was a house near Brixton – one of the few that hasn't been done up or turned into flats. I had to turn it into a workable location by taking a wall out and putting a kitchen in. We made the posters ourselves in the art department to avoid being sued. The same went for the banners in the anti-capitalists' demonstration.' In the story, the demo turns into a riot. 'We wanted to smash windows and burn cars but I was asking permission to do this in October 2001, which was a very sensitive time for anything to do with terrorism', says Rupert Bray. 'We had to temper it down and ended up in Croydon, rather than Central London.'

The riot scenes were some of the busiest for prop master Peter Hallam. 'There were over 100 protestors, each of whom had either a banner, drum, whistle, mask or claxon. The 50 or so riot police were each fully dressed with a weapons belt, baton, shield and radio. These all had to be handed out and collected at the start and end of each sequence

A demo scene involved over 150 props – and each one had to be counted in and out.

throughout the day. Experience tells us that supporting artists have been known to misplace their props whilst having a cup of tea, so to alleviate the ensuing panic and delay, the standbys made a full list of who had what and checked them off each time. No lunch break for the prop boys that day! What looks like mayhem on the screen is in fact a meticulously thought-out procedure between the art department and special effects crew. This ensures the utmost safety at all times, whilst still retaining all the drama and excitement.'

For director Diarmuid Lawrence, the second script presented a chance to show another side of the SAS. 'Episode one is very dramatic but amongst the work the SAS most famously does best is being invisible. They have been known to dig their way into the eaves of a house and sit there not re-supplied for three months. This requires extraordinary patience and stamina but it's not really the stuff of drama. However, we wanted to depict their undercover work in episode two. It's a good story because the sense of a monumental gun going wild gives the validation to involve the SAS rather than Special Branch.'

Tom Clegg took over as director for the second block, covering episodes three and four. He says: 'I tried to keep a semi-documentary feel to the filming because it's not really a sedentary, beautifully-composed watch. *Ultimate Force* is in total contrast to my last job filming rural 1900s England for *My Uncle Silas*. The problem is that the SAS exist and are in the news. We know about their methods and the type of people they are. You are setting yourselves up dramatically where people are able to judge you and compare with the reality.' Tom is no newcomer to military dramas, however, having previously directed *Bravo Two Zero* and 14 episodes of *Sharpe*. 'For *Bravo Two Zero* I stayed as close to the event as I could and I tried to do the same for *Ultimate Force*. Our business is to create drama so we are not into total reality, but we want to do it well and so do the actors. When they put on the gear and handle the guns and ammunition, you can see the excitement in their eyes. The real SAS soldiers get the same excitement because their training is all about that moment. It's like directing – if you don't get a few butterflies you might as well give up.'

Tom's episodes see Red Troop involved in the selection of new SAS recruits before being sent to a laboratory where terrorists break in to steal an anthrax mutation. 'The selection episode sees the soldiers swimming across a strong current. We could have done it from the riverbank but we took the camera in a dinghy and went alongside them. The closer the camera appears, the greater the sense of involvement. But it was tricky because time is a big factor. A feature film would get a week to shoot what we had to achieve in a day. Luckily our cameraman Kevin Rowley is happy to muck in and he

Director Tom Clegg checks a camera shot in the anthrax laboratory.

makes people laugh. When it's the middle of winter and we all have to get in the freezing water, believe me, that's important! In reality the SAS would have swum across the river naked with their clothes in a plastic bag above them. We would have done that except it was February and we are very much bound by nudity. The actors also had wet suits under their uniforms because we didn't want them to get pneumonia.'

SAS selection normally takes place in the Brecon Beacons in Wales. Rupert Bray contacted the Forestry Commission to help him find a suitable alternative venue. 'I knew that Wales was fairly aggressive countryside with blocks of conifers and the Forestry Commission told me what they had in the Home Counties. We ended up with Bourne Woods in Farnham, which was the same place used for the opening scene of the film *Gladiator*. Unfortunately there is no white water in the Home Counties so we filmed the river scenes at Sonning Weir. It rained constantly and the Thames was the highest it had been for months.'

One of the props required from Peter Hallam in episode three was a telephone box. 'We sited it alongside the roadway in a forest. But when we returned the following day, we were greeted by a member of the public complaining that the telephone didn't work. I had to explain!

'Episode four looks dangerous, but the exploding glass laboratory equipment was, in fact, made of resin, the spilling caustic liquids were water, food thickener and vegetable dyes, and Ross's blood came from a theatrical supplier'. Finding a building to use as a laboratory involved three separate locations. 'At Upper Heyford, the Americans had everything — a bowling alley, a supermarket and a hospital, and luckily the hospital operating rooms were perfect for our lab. We cleaned it up to make it more high-tech. It didn't have everything we needed so we used a disused office block in Brentford as the foyer, plus a waterworks in Iver for the exterior', explains Gary Williamson. 'It was complicated to mix the three locations, doubly so because a lot of the episode is on closed-circuit TV. I did a ground plan and there was an art director with the camera who could point out which way they could and couldn't shoot, so it worked fine on film.'

Adds Rupert Bray: 'At the Three Valleys Water plant we had to ensure that there was no signage connecting it to anthrax. It was a great location with a large turbine hall where the SAS come off a mobile crane before coming through a ventilation capsule and abseiling down. The surroundings were stark and surreal.'

As *Ultimate Force* entered the final block of filming, there was no let up for the production team. With just two episodes to go, they were challenged to create Ireland — both North and South — and Bosnia. Time was also proving a pressure for co-creator Rob Heyland, who was working on all six episodes, so actor and scriptwriter Len Collin and Julian Jones were brought in to write episode five.

'Rob had a tentative idea about setting an episode in Northern Ireland which I used as the basis for the story', explains Len. 'I was brought up in County Sligo, which is not far from the border, and I lived there for about five years as a child. I was in Ireland when Louis Mountbatten was murdered and I've spent a lot of time in the border towns, so it was an area I knew something about. The area in Easkey where Bobby Sands was buried helped in terms of creating the psyche of the place. I have very strong views on Northern Ireland so I had a theme to get across. In Ireland, in general, everyone is wrong. I wanted to encapsulate that. There is a line in the script when the Special Branch officer says "In Ireland we like to play penny whistles and bang the drum", meaning very little really gets done. I think that's true.' Len and Rob talked at length about the characters. 'They are not clichés – I know those types of characters do exist. I used to write for *Soldier Soldier* and I live in Colchester now, which is an army town. Rob and I clicked straight away and Chris Ryan helped me a lot. The good guys are allowed to be bad in *Ultimate Force*. That really appealed to me and it's more grown up than a lot of television.'

Len wasn't the only one with an inside knowledge of Irish society – production designer Gary Williamson comes from Belfast. 'I know the difference between the north and the south, between Protestant and Catholic, and it's very subtle. When we went into pubs, I knew if they didn't feel right. We wanted to use an Irish cottage as the safe house where Jamie is held and tortured but the architecture around the M25 is wrong. Instead we decided to go for bland and settled on a mobile home – on the premise that inside a boring, normal-looking place, something awful is going on.'

Adds Gary: 'My mum and dad still live in Bangor and I visited them and took photographs to make sure the licence plates and Land Rovers covered in mesh looked right. And my art director is from the south, so he got some Harp flown over for our pub and persuaded his dad to photograph Irish police cars and road signs so we could make up our own.' As well as car number plates for the North and South, every detail had to be thought of, including washable graffiti. There was even an Irish Yellow Pages imported especially.

For locations, Slough doubled up as Belfast, while the vehicle checkpoint near the border where Jamie is kidnapped was staged at the Transport Research

A violent kidnap set in Northern Ireland had to be filmed on private roads

Bosnia was created in Wendover Woods and an abandoned sawmill near Pinewood Studios.

Laboratory at Crowthorne. Rupert Bray explains: 'To film a shoot-out and kidnap on a public road would have been a nightmare but the Transport Research Laboratory has its own road system which is used for testing all kinds of things. We could film as much violence, fast driving, Northern Irish uniforms and firing guns as we wanted to. And because the area was covered in conifers and bog, it could pass as Northern Ireland.'

Creating Bosnia for the final episode seemed an impossible challenge at first. 'When I first read the script for episode six I thought we would never do it. We had to avoid anything that felt like England – no red brick, no trees like oak. But surprisingly it turned out to be fairly easy', says Rupert. Gary adds: 'We'd seen Wendover Woods when we were looking for a location to film the selection episode. It wasn't right for Wales but it is a gorgeous valley which doesn't look at all English. We took the director Tim Leandro there and he loved it. Having got the approaches sorted, we just needed to find the village. We looked for a 1920s or 30s factory which we could bomb damage, but there were none on their own. Then we thought of a sawmill, which the militia might have taken over for their encampment. Amazingly we found one right next to Pinewood in Black Park. A company had gone bankrupt, leaving a lot of good set dressing like old cars and abandoned burned-out vehicles. We had to dress it like an inn and put in windows and doors so we could blow them out. It did look convincing.'

Prop master Peter Hallam was required to build a two-lane road from a horse track for the roadblock scene. 'This involved us laying 35 tons of Grade 1 top stone along a 200 metre stretch and because the location was so remote we had to use wheelbarrows, shovels and rakes instead of heavy plant equipment. The one thing you don't want at times like those is bad weather – but of course it rained all day!'

Tim Leandro, who directed episodes five and six, was delighted with the attention to authentic detail. 'In both episodes our guest cast were utterly convincing. In episode five they were Irish and in our Bosnia episode they were real Serbs. When we haven't got the budget to go abroad, it's details like those, which make the difference. Plus we were very lucky with the weather – it poured down in Ireland and was glorious sunshine when we were filming in Bosnia!'

Ultimate Force was a baptism of fire for Tim, whose credits include *London's Burning*, *Casualty* and *Justice in Wonderland*. 'I've never worked with gunfire before so it was a steep learning curve for me. We had to change a couple of shots because some of the things I originally wanted would have put the actors in positions of extreme danger. For me, moving into the world of the SAS was very challenging. I think they are superhuman and I felt a great responsibility to get it right and make their world believable. But it's a fine line. The professionalism must not be so great that it outstrips their humanity. I think the great thing about *Ultimate Force* is that there are big sequences and more intimate ones too. One day you've got this massive shoot-out in Bosnia and another day you're very contained, in a safe house in the Irish Republic. Another day we had an interesting scene with Twamley at home. It showed him in a completely different situation but still the SAS didn't leave him.'

Tim also appreciates the efforts of DOP and camera operator Kevin Rowley, who kept going through five months of 12-hour action-packed days in order to capture the intimate style of camerawork chosen for the series. Kevin, however, has plenty of experience of life in the firing line, having spent more than 20 years as a BBC cameraman working in news and current affairs, before moving on to work on dramas such as *Between The Lines* and *Poirot*. 'I started in Londonderry in 1968 and also went to south-east

Director Tim Leandro learns about gunfire from Chris Ryan.

Asia, India and Africa with *Panorama*. If you've covered war zones you never forget it. You wash that bit of your life away and start again. Now I think "cut", but when you're in a war zone you can't say "cut" and go home. You can recreate people dying, but if you've seen people dying it sticks with you.

'*Ultimate Force* has been very hard work, standing up all day with a hand-held camera, often in the rain with people getting coughs and colds. It's sheer madness but I love it.'

FIREPOWER

Ear-splitting fire fights, enormous explosions sending bodies flying and bullet wounds pumping with blood – *Ultimate Force* takes no prisoners when it comes to special effects. During the course of filming the series, 10,000 rounds of ammunition were fired. Dramatic shootouts and exciting action sequences are a big part of the drama but those electric moments that flash before the eyes on screen have to be carefully choreographed with weeks of planning by the behind-the-scenes crew. Creating the firepower for *Ultimate Force* is a team effort, largely between the armourer, stunt co-ordinator and special effects co-ordinator, working with the directors to make sure the scenes have the desired amount of smoke, loud bangs, bullets and blood – without excessive violence and gore.

As ever, all this has to be achieved within the limitations of a TV budget. With viewers used to a diet of Hollywood movies where millions of dollars are spent on effects alone, the crew work hard to deliver show-stopping images at a fraction of the cost. Producer Peter Norris explains: 'It's a bit like a military campaign. We had to plan the action sequences and visual effects meticulously because we had a limited amount of time and money to spend on them. So it's essential that we used good people.'

Sourcing a weapon for a television production is not like finding any other prop. The industry is closely regulated and firearms supply companies have to be approved by the Home Office. The contract for *Ultimate Force* went to Perdix, a company whose other credits include *Gosford Park*,

Preston Front, *The Bill*, *Scarlet Pimpernel* and *All The King's Men*.

General manager Greg Pearson researched weapons favoured by the SAS, including the Heckler & Koch MP5 submachine gun, the Sig Sauer pistol and the M16 combat rifle. The series also features a wider array of firearms, such as Berettas, Makarov pistols, AK47s and an Accuracy International sniper's rifle, which are used by Red Troop's terrorist targets. Says Greg: 'The SAS use quite a small group of weapons and ammunition, but they have to be confident and competent with the ones everybody else uses. Part of the training is being able to recognize what the bad guys are using to shoot at them, so they know if they can hide safely behind a tree or behind a steel plate. **AND IF THEY PICK UP A GUN ON THE BATTLEFIELD, THEY HAVE TO KNOW HOW TO USE IT.**' Armourers Tack Baldwin and Frank Brown were responsible for getting the chosen weapons to the locations, training the actors how to use them – and, most importantly, ensuring their safety.

Although only blank, rather than live, ammunition is used, injuries or even death could still occur. There is also potential danger from grenade launchers on guns because the cases fly out to the side when they are fired. And the sound of repeated gunfire can injure hearing – so all the crew are supplied with earplugs or ear defenders. In addition to the real firearms, Perdix provided rubber pistols and guns to use when characters are pistol-whipped. Explains Tack: 'The actors are supposed to be SAS guys with several years' experience of military work. We have

Submachine guns are part of the trooper's kit – and they're not afraid to use them.

to train them so it looks like second nature. We watch all the time and keep correcting them and retraining them on each particular piece of kit, so they look professional. Obviously Chris Ryan is fantastically *au fait* with weapons and him being on set has helped a lot.

'It's a constant counting of rounds and a constant vigil. In one scene at the Bosnian camp we had 25 weapons being used so safety is crucial. **EVEN IMITATION WEAPONS ARE CLASSED AS OFFENSIVE WEAPONS** so we do not take any chances. But we try to let the actors handle the weapons a lot because it helps them get used to them and look better on screen.' Frank says: 'As soon as the director shouts "cut" we leap into action to get all the weapons back and count them in. People do tend to wander off on a film set and forget they are walking around with a gun. On a big set like this when you've got eight main actors with M16s and the baddies running around with AK47s it's a legal requirement to have two armourers.'

Tack adds: 'We try to give the director what he wants. We read the script and see how they set the shot up, then we alter it for safety. Even if there's a very slight element of danger we just stop the shoot. Then we work with the crew to come up with a different solution.' Thanks to their experience in films, the armourers know it is still possible to

Armourer Frank Brown (right) is vigilant whenever guns are in use.

create dramatic shots safely. In *Ultimate Force*, when guns appear to be firing directly at the camera, director of photography Kevin Rowley was covered in thick canvas and supplied with soft ear plugs, ear defenders and headphones, while Frank and Tack held armoured shields around him.

The job is far from done when the crew 'wrap' at the end of a 12-hour day. Tack says: 'Each weapon is signed out to a particular artist and when we wrap in the evening and travel back to our base, we still have at least an hour and a half of cleaning, logging serial numbers, booking weapons back in and registering them. Our van might have 18 fully automatic machine guns on it, worth up to £1,000 a piece, along with blank ammunition, although this is kept in separate locked boxes. So we have satellite tracking fitted and the vehicle is registered with the police. The Home Office guidelines are very strict. We don't stop for anyone and we're not allowed to get out of the vehicle on a public road.' Most Perdix armourers have a military background – Tack himself served with the Parachute Regiment for four years. 'Some people think armourers are gun freaks but we're quite normal and hard-working. It's actually very tiring work because you can never go on to automatic pilot. You have to be on the ball all the time and know where everything is.'

Alongside the guns and ammunition come the bangs and explosions – the work of special effects co-ordinator Tony Harding and his team. 'We do everything that no-one else can do', laughs Tony. 'If a scene is potentially dangerous or not straightforward they call us in. We could be asked to

Special effects co-ordinator Tony Harding (left) is in charge of spectacular images such as explosions and bullet holes.

make rain or floods but for *Ultimate Force* it's all been to do with killing. The director always wants a spectacle and it's up to us to make sure it is safe.' Tony describes his work as 'technical trickery' and it can be seen right from the beginning of *Ultimate Force*. 'It all started off with the Killing House. We blew in the door and in bursts the SAS then we blew two windows in. We had bullet hits on people and objects, including one of the soldiers blowing out the screen of a TV. The trick is to do all this without injuring anyone. **TO BLOW WINDOWS IN WE USE COMPRESSED AIR AS THE MAIN FORCE**. The air comes from a cannon, which is a

big funnel connected to an air bottle and it blasts out 100lb of air per second. It's pretty instant and will blow anything out of the way. To make it look like an explosion and not just a blast of air, we put a small pyrotechnic charge in front of it so you get flame and smoke at the same time.'

Tony works with the make-up department to create bullet wounds. 'Bullet hits are a filmic effect because in reality when a bullet hits someone you don't see the entry wound. But in *Ultimate Force*, the directors have always wanted gory entry wounds as well as exit wounds, usually coupled with lots of blood being sprayed over the nearest wall. We use a small custom-made pyrotechnic device which sits on a stainless steel plate and is put in between the actor's body and his costume. It is then fired electrically on cue to show where the bullet has hit. In some instances we were doing up to six bullet wounds on an individual person – because the SAS don't just fire once!

'We had plenty of variation creating gunshot wounds on the actors. In one instance, Sam Leonard is shot in the leg. It was a severe bleeder, so we had a device that would pump blood out. It was a container of artificial blood with a tube running out of it, which the make-up artist disguised to look like a wound. We pumped the container at the other end to control the blood flow and I think it looked pretty dramatic.

'For the shoot out in the car in Northern Ireland, we had to create bullets ripping across a Land Rover.

A missile blows up a war criminal's hideout in Bosnia – thanks to pyrotechnics and compressed air.

On a metal object you have to make the bullet holes first, then put small charges behind each one and disguise them. The charges are fired in rapid succession to match the speed of a machine gun. So it's magic really.

'The last big special effect was a missile going into a cantina in Bosnia. The subsequent explosion was enormous and at the same time we had a stunt artist coming through the window. Once again, the director wanted an enormous explosion but we didn't want to hurt the stuntman. We used directional compressed air to take the force away and a small explosive charge again to create the flame and smoke. We work very closely with the stuntmen and I know a lot of them. It takes a long time to rig things like bullet holes and the rehearsals can take anything up to an hour, but the setting up time is important because we normally only get one go at it. When we were working at Waddesdon Manor we had to blow up two enormous vases of flowers right next to the main entrance. We had special vases made up of soft plaster so we had to get it right on the first take.'

Tony has lent his talents to a number of different programmes, including *Jonathan Creek*, *A Sword of Honour*, *The Worst Witch* and *Urban Gothic*. He has also worked with Bentley Productions on *Midsomer Murders*. 'For *Midsomer Murders* the deaths are not as graphic because it is pre-watershed, but for *Ultimate Force* the opposite seems to apply. It doesn't have a *Saving Private Ryan* budget so we have had to work hard to keep the standard up, with less time and money. We have tried to achieve feature-film effects on a television budget. The gory effects never turn my stomach because I think of it as another technical trick. When I watch films I always analyse the special effects and work out how they're done. I drive my wife mad because I say "there's a car crash coming any second" because I've recognized the stunt men!'

Tony turned to compressed air once again to help director Diarmuid Lawrence get the best effect for a scene in episode two. Diarmuid says: 'We had to fabricate the sense of a bullet missing a man's head by an inch or so. The bullet is fired from a sniper's rifle - the sort that was causing mayhem in Northern Ireland up until the ceasefire. **IT CAN KILL FROM THREE MILES AND GOES THROUGH BODY ARMOUR.** If it hits anyone, they're very likely to die of shock wherever they are hit. I had to give the sense of something as big as that going past a man's face. We tried to distort his face with a fan but it didn't have anything like the right amount of power. Eventually we used a compressed air ram to fire a shot of air with enormous power into this poor man's face. It distorted his cheeks, like someone on a big dipper. We had to be careful there was no grit in it or it could damage his sight. The stunt man showed him it was all right and then he took it like a man. I was very pleased with the result.'

Stunt co-ordinator Colin Skeaping employed more than 25 stuntmen and women for *Ultimate Force*. 'Our role in the production is to make the action sequences look realistic and the actors look tough and capable. The actor wants to portray the character as good at his job, brave and efficient – we make him look it. We also choreograph the fight sequences, show the actors how to punch and to fall, all in order to make it look realistic. Although I'm also a stuntman myself, my main job now is to make sure it is being shot in the right way.

'Every single episode of *Ultimate Force* required three or four days a week of stunts. There was always action, a lot of fights, people being shot and guys coming out of the window. Blowing people out of buildings takes a long time to set up. I use an air ram. The stuntman walks or runs onto it and as they do so it catapults them into the air – then they land on the mattress the other side. I employed a high number of stunt artists on the series for their various areas of expertise. Also, they have to resemble the actors to get away with it. One specialist stunt was free climbing up the side of a building, but we've also had storming a bank and blowing out windows, abseiling into buildings, dropping on to rooftops and coming through skylights. We had Ross Kemp dangling out of a helicopter for one episode. He was roped in to ensure his safety, but it looks very effective. In other scenes the actors and stuntmen were dressed in black combats, so you can't tell the difference between them, especially when they are wearing a respirator.'

Ten thousand rounds of blank ammunition were used in filming – with sound effects often added afterwards.

Working as a stunt double is not glamorous, as Colin explains. 'The stuntman who is doubling is not normally known in his own right; he can work continuously year after year without anyone recognizing him. You have to be very fit, not because you need to expend a lot of energy, but because you have to crash around, fall and bounce. Fitness is essential to take that kind of punishment, and, should you be injured, your fitness will help you recover more quickly.'

However, the cast were keen to get a slice of the action sequences themselves. Producer Peter Norris says: 'They are all macho boys who want to do all they can. They do jumping and anything to do with weapon firing and changing magazines because we've taught them how. We use stuntmen only when we're doing something the actor can't do or where he would be in danger. I encouraged the cast to get involved, but it had to be within reason. The last thing we needed was one of them to get hurt.' Tom Clegg, who directed episodes three and four, adds: 'None of the actors are pussycats and it was difficult for them to let the stunt guys take over sometimes. Actors love a physical challenge and they were determined to make it look good. In Iver, where we filmed Red Troop storming a chemical plant, the stunt guys were shinning up and down 40ft ropes. Everyone wanted to have a go that day – not just the actors but the crew as well.

'A GOOD DAY WOULD BE EXPLOSIONS, FIRE, STUNT MEN AND HAND-TO-HAND FIGHTING. It's not usually exciting getting guys shooting each other at long distance, but once you get to a closer shot you want to do it well. Chris Ryan has years of training but it's a different thing to bring in a new actor and lift him to an acceptable level in such specific skills. Some actors find props like cups of tea difficult to manage when they're doing dialogue. But in this they need a natural aptitude and a high level of physical fitness to move with the same style as a trained SAS trooper. It's full credit to the actors that you don't notice that on screen.'

Stunts, weapons and special effects are all expensive parts of a production and it was the job of line producer Ian Strachan to make sure all these costs were kept within the budget. 'On episodes five and six alone we used between six and eight thousand rounds of blanks. That was the most by miles because there were huge fire fights, but we used around 10,000 over all – at a cost of 60 pence a round. It's special ammo, made to bang and to flash, so you pay a lot of money for it.

'A good part of the budget had to go on effects, stunt doubles, guns and ammunition. But hardware like helicopters is also fiendishly expensive. We couldn't get them in military livery and the only people that have the big ones like Chinooks are the Ministry of Defence. Instead we used an Augusta 109 which is a machine the SAS like because it's a bit like the sports car of the helicopter world – a fast six-seater. It is painted jet black with no markings on it so it looks very good. I had to ask questions early and flag up areas where we would need special things like tanks. I got pictures of the weapons to see what everyone in Red Troop would need before going on

The Augusta 109 – the sports car of the helicopter world.

to the other characters. It has to look right and be reasonably authentic. Luckily the experts on this job made sure it was effective. Although it's storytelling, people take a pride in what they do. It would be wrong of me to say "you can't have those guns because they're going to cost another 20 quid". And

it makes the actor better if he's properly kitted out.'

Ian's role also encompassed health and safety. 'A statutory risk assessment is done and the crew responsible for the hazardous stuff also perform a risk assessment. Then you action what is necessary, be it crash mats and pads for stunt men or goggles and ear defenders for the crew. The barn used in episode six had been used as a garage so there was a potential fire hazard. We brought in a private fire service to check that all the pumps and fuel had gone and they also stood by on the day. The potential for going wrong on a series like this is immense. When you create fireballs you are chucking large amounts of propane gas and debris at people. You want to make sure there's a safe working distance but it still looks good. To do a major ITV action series safely and to come out of it on time is something I think everyone should be very proud of.'

The use of ammunition also had an impact on location manager Rupert Bray. 'There were many days when weapons were on display or firing. For a country that is not weapons-oriented, that is quite difficult. We had to inform the authorities and police and use our diplomatic skills with the public. It was a bit tricky when we were filming on public streets and we had a few local farmers complain that we were frightening the birds off. We filmed at a school in one episode and had to keep a machine gun away from 400 children. People that live around them all the time get used to them, but we obviously took every step to ensure the children were protected.'

Ultimate Force is a post-watershed show – but the use of guns and violence was an important matter of discussion between executive producer Brian True-May and bosses at the ITV Network Centre. Brian explains: 'When I sold the concept to ITV, I said "how far do we go in shooting people?" They said they wanted the reality so that's exactly what we've given

them. When the SAS are told to make hard arrests that means take no prisoners.'

Writer Rob Heyland believes it was the right decision to make. 'I think it's very brave of ITV to make something harsh. The reality of violence, particularly gun violence, is not very pretty. **THE SMELL OF BLOOD, THE ATMOSPHERE OF FEAR AND PANIC** – all of this is so ugly. At least ITV has had the courage to try and get somewhere towards it, rather than making a bunch of pretty boys going round and killing people like *The A Team*. I thought *The A Team* was great of its type and of its time but it's not what *Ultimate Force* is about. And to remind me, I have written above my desk "not *The A Team*".'

Even so, Rob is certain that the reality of the SAS's fight against terrorism is much harsher than the picture painted by the series. 'The SAS's attitude to life and death is very black and superficial. In episode two a man gets shot with a heavy-duty rifle. It goes through him and shoots a hole in the wall behind him. We were discussing it and what would actually happen is that his lungs would have been sucked out of his back. In the real-life incident that inspired that sequence, one of the SAS men leant over the body and said "oh, he looks like a 40-a-day man" then moved on. I accept that might have been pushing it a bit. We also toned down a scene in episode one when Henno shoots one of the bank robbers, which I had originally done as more of a blatant execution, but it's still pretty graphic. When the cops come in afterwards and each soldier is standing there with a body at his feet, Ricky Mann is wonderfully phlegmatic. I was frightened that I would be made to

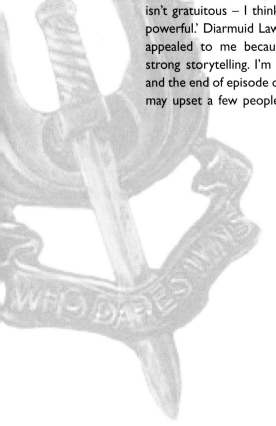

write something frothy, so I was pleased with the result, even though we compromised a bit.'

Violence was a major consideration for the directors, too. Tim Leandro, who directed episodes five and six, says: 'Usually on a production, someone like Brian True-May comes up and tells us we can't do this or that, but no-one has. We've had torture, sieges and enormous gun battles. I always shoot the scene in a way that gives us choices in editing, but the violence is intrinsic to the being of the people in the programme. You couldn't make a programme about the SAS and have them being soft. It's probably the most violent thing I've ever seen on telly but it isn't gratuitous – I think it's startling and incredibly powerful.' Diarmuid Lawrence adds: 'Ultimate Force appealed to me because it's very tight and very strong storytelling. I'm not wildly fond of violence and the end of episode one is reasonably graphic and may upset a few people. But I think it's quite right because it does reflect the military aspect of the SAS, which is "we're not really here to put handcuffs on people, we're here to shoot people who started shooting first". That is the reality and it wouldn't be right to portray them in any other way. I know the ITV Network Centre want our heroes to be heroes, but they are not heroes in the sense of London's Burning. They're not people who break into buildings to save others, they are people who, necessarily for us, occasionally break into buildings to shoot others. They are rescuing people at the same time, but you can't equate their work with the other services.'

Adds Diarmuid: 'It's good for an audience to be confronted with that. We're all glad to have the SAS there. The Parachute Regiment, where a lot of them are recruited from, may not be my idea of a fun Saturday night out with the boys, but they are the dogs of war and everybody needs them. I'd rather have them on my side than somebody else's.'

WEAPONS USED BY RED TROOP

MP5 A submachine gun made by Heckler & Koch, the MP5 has become a symbol of anti-terrorist forces all round the world. It is reliable, controllable and accurate, with single shot, automatic and trigger burst firing capability, using 9mm bullets. It is used by Red Troop on many of their missions. Over 120 variants of the HK MP5 are available – in Northern Ireland, Caroline uses the MP5K – a short version.

SIG The Sig Sauer P226 is carried by the SAS along with a larger weapon, such as the MP5, depending on the requirements of the job. A 9mm Swiss-made pistol with an excellent record for accuracy, the Sig is a self-loading handgun, with a 15-round magazine. It offers the SAS rapid readiness for combat as there is no manually-operated safety catch. Discharge can only occur by pulling the trigger, which also locks the action of the weapon.

M16 A popular combat rifle of the SAS, which can be combined with a 203 grenade launcher clipped underneath. Manufactured by Colt, it offers single shot and automatic capability, using 5.56 calibre bullets in rounds of 30. The M16 operates in all conditions and is suitable for use at close range and in open spaces. At nearly 40 inches in length, it is quite a long rifle in its standard configuration. A shorter version, the Carbine, is also used by Red Troop.

Walther PPK Made famous by James Bond, this baby gun measures 4ins by just over 6ins and weighs 21oz. It is small enough to fit in a pocket – or even in Caroline's knickers in episode six. The Walther PPK is used with a small bullet, the .32 ACP. It can be used with a suppressor or small silencer, which suppresses the sound of the bullet's movement through the air.

SA80 The standard personal weapon issued to British Army soldiers. The Regiment prefers to use the M16, but the SA80 is used when the SAS is operating undercover as a regular army soldier, to blend in. In Northern Ireland, Red Troop also use the HK53, which has the same 5.56 ammunition as the standard British rifle but offers greater power.

LAW66 The rocket launcher used by Red Troop in Bosnia is an LAW or Light Antitank Weapon, sending a high-explosive rocket on to a target.

Stun Grenade Also known as a flashbang, a stun grenade combines extremely loud noise with very bright light and disorientates anyone in close proximity when it goes off. It gives the SAS vital seconds while terrorists are unable to move.

Shotguns 870 Remington pump action shotguns feature in the Killing House when Red Troop blow hinges off doors. The guns generally fire a solid slug bullet but can use gas as well. Shotguns can be fitted with a bungee rig so, once used, they can be let go, enabling the trooper to use another weapon quickly.

WEAPONS USED BY RED TROOP'S ENEMIES

AK47 Manufactured by Kalashnikov, the AK47 was the standard infantry weapon of many communist regimes and remains popular. An assault rifle, it is extremely robust and will operate under almost any conditions, firing a 7.62mm round. It is also relatively cheap. The AK47 is used by enemies of Red Troop, especially in Bosnia.

AW50F The Accuracy International .50 is an extremely powerful sniping rifle. Used in the Gulf by Special Forces, it is accurate even over distances of 3kms. Firing a half-inch bullet, the AW50F weighs 35lb without ammunition, measures 4ft 6ins long but has a folding butt. It can be used with a normal bullet, a tracer bullet with red dot tail, a high velocity bullet or an incendiary round, which could go into a fuel tank and then explode. Red Troop discovers this weapon is being used by an anti-capitalist group in episode two, and Jamie has to use his sniping skills in an attempt to retrieve it.

Makarov A Russian pistol, which flooded the market after the break-up of the Soviet bloc. It carries a 9mm short round and is used by the Chechen terrorists at the laboratory in episode four and by Glasnovic in Bosnia in episode six.

Beretta 92 A big 9mm handgun which is popular all over the world, with a combination of powerful firing, precision, safety and reliability. Red Troop finds it in the hands of Moussa, one of the Chechens who break into the laboratory in search of a lethal anthrax mutation, in episode four.

CZ75 A Czechoslovakian 9mm all-steel, semi-automatic, double-action pistol, offering high accuracy and long service. Sean Maguire, one of the gang that kidnaps Jamie, carries the CZ75 in episode five.

Glock 18 A Swedish-made gun, also used by the terrorists in Northern Ireland. The Glock 18 is fully automatic – a pistol that works like a machine gun and empties its magazine in 2.2 seconds, creating a large flash.

Minimi An unusual 5.56 calibre light machine-gun which can be used with a disintegrating belt or a standard M16 magazine. It is popular with American Special Forces and is one of the weapons in Glasnovic's armoury in episode six.

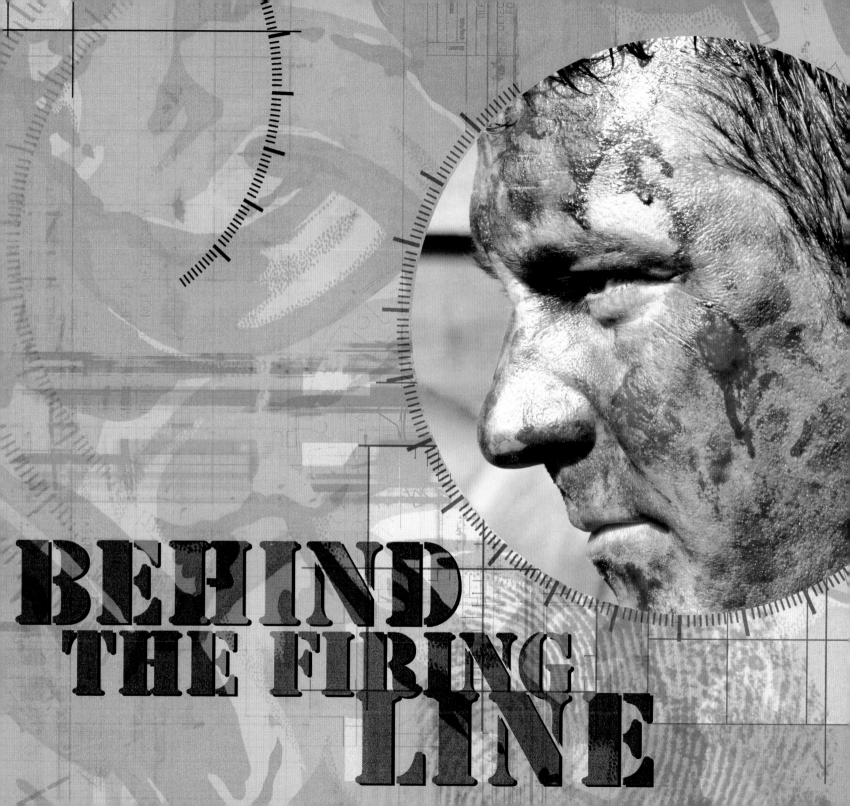

BEHIND THE FIRING LINE

Bringing *Ultimate Force* to the screen involved upwards of 100 people. The majority of the crew worked on location during the months of shooting, others manned Bentley's production office, while in another corner the post-production team assembled the sound and pictures to make the finished episodes. Skills from accountancy to continuity and from script editing to sound all play their part, but perhaps particular credit should go to the work of the make-up and costume teams, who created the look of Red Troop – then messed up their hard work with some terrible 'injuries'.

Vanessa Johnson is the make-up designer – but her kit for the job had a few extra essential supplies on top of the powders, lipsticks and hairspray. 'The biggest requirement on Ultimate Force was blood. Lots of it – dry blood, runny blood, thick blood, congealed blood, clotting blood, fresh blood – anything you can think of. I went through so much of the stuff **I HAD TO GET A WINE BOX OF BLOOD WITH A TAP ON IT!** The blood is supplied by a specialist company. You tell them what you want and they make it up for you. In the past, we used to make up our own, but now it's a very big market. I also had scar material which you paint on the skin. It tightens as it dries to pull the skin in, like a scar. Then there were bruise palettes with all the different colours needed for bruises, and bruising gel, which you can put over the top to make it shiny. It's a whole field on its own.'

Despite the distinctly unglamorous nature of the job, Vanessa enjoyed the challenge of creating bullet wounds and other injuries. 'We've been allowed to be very graphic. We have books and picture references of what the wounds would really look like, and Chris Ryan has shown us a few horrible, but useful, pictures of injuries. Gerry Savage, the unit nurse, also explained it to us from a medical point of view, but then you've got a director calling "more blood, more blood". So that's what we give them. You have to learn what sort of guns will make what sort of wounds, then use a bit of artistic licence in order to adapt the injury to what people expect. For example, facial bullet wounds are really only a hole in the head at the front. It's at the back

Make-up designer Vanessa Johnson uses a pot of fake blood on an "injured" soldier.

that you get the splatter. People think the whole of the face gets blown off but only certain types of guns will do that. It's been a fascinating experience coming so close to weapons and explosions that most of your life you would never come near, thank goodness. Sometimes your ears are ringing and there's a trembling in your whole body with all the guns going off.'

Vanessa and make-up artist Jill Conway arrived on the *Ultimate Force* set early to get the cast ready to start filming at 8 am. 'My policy has always been that before seven, faces aren't ready to be made up. They're still sleepy and don't want to have make-up put on them, male or female. When you're doing a big period drama, you have to, and we did a couple of times when we had huge crowd calls, but we try very hard not to start before seven.'

Vanessa and Jill often had more than 15 members of cast to make-up and check throughout the filming day. 'I look after Ross and Jamie but we've mixed and matched. It is very busy but we go into a brilliant routine when they arrive. It's like a conveyor belt – they come on the make-up van, get made up and go off and have breakfast. Then we check and tidy them up during the day as necessary', says Vanessa. 'It's been a hard shoot and we've had the van parked in some pretty bleak places. We've also had some fairly horrible days when we've been absolutely saturated. The actors look good, but we're dripping wet. But we've all had such fun.'

Vanessa's make-up truck became a popular place for the cast to congregate between scenes. 'They all come in and visit the make-up bus. We've

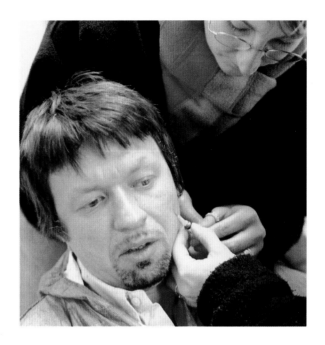

Chechen terrorist Moussa is hit in the cheek by a syringe – in reality it was attached painlessly by the make-up team.

got our coffee machine going at one end and the actors come in to make their tea and coffee or a Berocca vitamin drink if they're hung over. Alex Reid even baked cakes and biscuits for us on her days off and that brought even more people on to the bus!'

Vanessa had a battle with the male actors on one subject, though – shaving. 'Some of the younger actors wanted to look stubbly but it's just not done. It's the one thing Chris Ryan told us time and time again. To get into the SAS you go through such a strict military training and part of it is the discipline of shaving. The troopers are very meticulous. When they are on a 30-minute call, they have to be clean shaven because gas masks don't work if there's stubble in the way. They would get gassed. That's just a little point that anybody in the know would pick up on immediately. It got to the point when one day I put a big notice up on the make-up door saying "yes, you have to shave". It became a bit of an on-going joke. It was my birthday during the shoot and the actors managed to find a card with a picture of a whale on it, and inside it said "save the whale, not shave the whale"!' To comply with Vanessa's strict shaving regime, all the male actors kept a bag on the make-up truck to hold their own shaver and other essentials, like a toothbrush. 'The other thing we had to keep on top of was their hair. We shoot out of order so it's important for continuity that there's not a sudden change in their hair length. Men's hair grows fast so we had to keep tipping the ends all the time.'

Shooting out of sequence was also difficult for scenes involving injuries. 'Bruises change colour every day, but we might shoot the day the bruise has almost gone first, then when it's at its worst. The beating itself can be last of all. When it comes to the fight you have to say where the person can be hit, in order to fit in with the bruising we've already done.' 'You try to work the action through with the director and actor, but on the day of filming things can change, especially in a fight scene. It can be tricky to keep the overall look going so we take lots of photographs.'

Although it was not possible for most scenes, Vanessa pleaded with the director to keep one

Actors had to shave diligently to ensure a proper fit for the respirator.

sequence in story order – the torture and beating of SAS trooper Jamie Dow in episode five. 'I begged them to shoot the torture in the right sequence. It's a story of Jamie's deterioration and it would have been a nightmare to create backwards, and impossible for the actor Jamie Draven as well. Fortunately they kept us on a path and it was a week's work creating that look every day, plus dyeing his hair and putting on a disguise, because he is impersonating someone when he is kidnapped. Jamie was in make-up for hours.'

Costume designer Reg Samuel and his team were responsible for creating the uniforms and clothes worn by Red Troop and their enemies, which was a complicated task involving detailed research – and the odd leap of faith. Abigail Hicks, a regular on Bentley Productions' other major drama, *Midsomer Murders*, was costume supervisor on the series and began work with less than a month to go before the first day of filming. 'We started off with the knowledge that the Ministry of Defence didn't want to co-operate with the series so we were doing it in the dark. With the help of Chris Ryan and some reference books we set about getting the costumes together.

'Each member of Red Troop has four sets of clothes. First there are the "blacks", which they wear on covert operations. It's basically an all-in-one boilersuit with a black jumper, a padded waistcoat and an assault vest that carries the bullets, grenades and gun attachments, along with a helmet and black

Uniforms, medals and insignia all required detailed research.

leather gloves. The boilersuits have a number on the sleeve to identify each person, because when they've got the balaclavas and respirators on they could be almost anyone. Their other uniform is the DPMs or camouflage. They have trousers and a green top and that's what they wear when they're in Ireland or Afghanistan. They have black Magnum boots, which are very comfortable and waterproof, and they wear them with the blacks and the DPMs. Each character has his own civvies. When a soldier joins the SAS, he is given an amount of money to buy bland, non-descript clothes. Within that, we have tried to reflect our characters – Jem is slightly flashy, while Jamie comes from a working-class background. They also have disguise civilian clothes for undercover work, whether they're pretending to be builders or people in smart suits.'

Each character has four main costume sets, but Abigail had to buy or hire three or four copies of each, due to the nature of *Ultimate Force*. 'Red Troop are always getting shot at or dirty so we have to make sure we buy things you can get more than one of. We shoot out of sequence, so you can start with them getting bloody, dirty and disgusting and then they have to look nice afterwards. The same goes for Caroline. She doesn't have a black outfit but she has a general selection of casual, comfortable clothes, jeans and jackets and a pair of Magnum boots, as well as an army uniform and DPMs. And when she has to pose as a doctor and

Characters end up dirty, bloody or dead so triplicate sets of clothing are needed.

Danny Sapani is helped into his DPMs – or camouflage gear – by the costume team.

a journalist, she needs outfits to match. There's not a lot of glamour because it's not that type of show.'

With so many characters and costume changes, there's never a dull moment. 'It's a very busy show and the whole cast is in most of the time', says Abigail. 'We've had two trucks, one for the main cast and the other for the guest outfits, be they Serbian, UN, British army, Northern Ireland police,

Garda, plus all the clothes for the baddies. Because Red Troop's enemies usually end up very dead with lots of bullet holes you have to have triples of everything. We work with special effects to do the bullet holes. They put a blood sac and electric charge behind the shirt and when the gun is fired, the charge is set off and the blood comes out. The force is usually enough to split the material but

sometimes you need to get the scissors out.' She adds: 'We have a washing machine, tumble drier and ironing board on the truck and we have to make sure there is a whole clean outfit ready all the time.'

Wardrobe master Gerald Moulin specializes in military uniforms for film and television. His work includes *Band of Brothers*, *Sharpe* and *Enemy at the Gate*. 'As soon as I heard about *Ultimate Force*, I approached Bentley and offered my services. It's quite a specialized area and I've built up my own reference library over the years. Having said that, **IT WAS A DIFFICULT JOB TRYING TO FIND REFERENCES ABOUT THE SAS BECAUSE THEY ARE SO SENSITIVE FOR SECURITY REASONS.** We created a facsimile of the counter revolutionary warfare uniform, which they wear when they go into the bank siege in episode one. Chris Ryan came in when we had everyone dressed in their black outfits and asked where we got the uniform from. That was great because we had done it ourselves.

'In order to get the right look for the helmets, we bought Dutch winter ones, which are like the American Kevlars but white, so we had to spray them black continually, because they kept chipping. Then just after I'd bought them the black ones started being imported!

'It was difficult for the actors to get used to the respirators, especially when they were in the close

Soldiers on SAS selection have to wear Second World War battledress.

confines of corridors filled with thick smoke. You can lose your way very easily and even the stuntmen had problems. The explosions went off and they came through the skylight but couldn't see what they were landing on. But it looks good.'

Some of the scenes required the actors to wear berets. 'I had to spend time shrinking the principals' berets and as many of the other actors as I could. I had two bowls, one of hot water and one of cold and would dunk the berets into each one for something like 40 seconds each way until they slowly shrank up. Then I'd mould each one on to my head and try to do slightly different shapes with each, before letting them dry for 24 hours. It was important to do that because some regiments have a very specific way of wearing their berets. We had to create up to 40 Paras within the series, but luckily we had a lot of ex-Paras as extras so they knew what to do and they helped the others.'

As well as the main cast, Gerald had his work cut out with uniforms for the other soldiers and police forces that feature in the series. 'We have motorbike police, foot patrol, police in cars and riot police and we've made up our own fake badges so we don't upset anyone. We've done French police at the chateau, the Garda in Eire and the Police Service of Northern Ireland. We sometimes read a script and found things we weren't expecting, like Serbians. There wasn't a lot of time or reference material available, but I did manage to have the Serbian badges reproduced. More and more these days, people are interested in uniforms, insignia and medals so you can't afford to be wrong.

But it's a drama for television, so you have to do the best you can within the budget.'

For episode three, 'Natural Selection', the soldiers on SAS selection were made to wear World War II battledress – jackets and trousers and heavy woollen overcoats. 'Luckily the uniform is still readily available, but we had to have three changes per person because they were getting soaked the whole time in the rain and by crossing the river. It was bucketing with rain the whole day but we looked after the actors by providing a hot tub. They would change for the stunts and they'd each have a turn in the warm water, stepping into the hot tub fully clothed. The scene in the river took a whole day to shoot but at the end everybody seemed quite happy. It was a sensible precaution to have the tub because you could get hypothermia. I would have quite liked to get in myself!'

Keeping an eye on the health and wellbeing of the cast and crew was unit nurse Gerry Savage. A former hospital staff nurse, trained and experienced in both accident and emergency and intensive-care work, Gerry joined the film industry after stand-by stints on *Carry On Columbus* and *The Bill*. His credits since include *Hornblower* and *Soldier Soldier*. 'On a quiet day there are between 70 and 80 people but when we get the full complement of extras it's 150. On a major day I call in another paramedic with an ambulance to help me. A lot of the job is preparation but you have to be ready to deal with the unexpected. Generally speaking, it's a case of keeping everyone going through the winter.

'There were a few coughs and colds but once something gets hold of the unit it can become like a mini epidemic. We supply vitamin supplements to keep their immune systems up. My kit is quite extensive – it goes from pills and potions to oxygen, neck braces and a nebuliser for asthmatics. On the action days I liaise with special effects and the stunt co-ordinator. One of the stunt men was very close to the mortar in a big explosion so I put some special fire retardant on his face, which was actually KY Jelly. It stops the flash flames from reaching the skin and prevents any scorch marks. But the pharmacist gave me a funny look when I asked for six tubes of it!'

Although Gerry describes *Ultimate Force* as a very safe shoot, considering the amount of fire and explosions, there were a couple of occasions when he needed to call upon his first-aid skills. 'Ross Kemp received a burn to his arm when he was hit by a spark from a special effect. Luckily it was very superficial. On another day Laurence Fox twisted his ankle quite badly when he was coming down a hill.' Gerry's skills were also used in front of the camera. 'I work with the make-up department when they're creating injuries, such as when Henno is shot in the laboratory and when Jamie is tortured. Also I helped when one of the troop is on a ventilator, by showing how to put a tube in – although obviously it only went into his mouth.' He even features as an extra in the series. 'There's a couple of scenes where I play an army paramedic. I used to be a territorial with the Royal Army Medical Corps so it's all very familiar. Now I'm a real medic playing a pretend medic and I'm a bit worried about getting typecast!'

Another important way of keeping the crew going through a long winter's shoot is good food, provided by specialist caterers Location Café. Line producer Ian Strachan says: 'We give the crew breakfast, lunch and afternoon tea. It's important to make sure they are well fed, especially in the cold weather. You get up in the dark and go home in the dark, so food is vital fuel. It's a long and hard day, but if they're well fed, at least that's one less thing to moan about. We had more than 80 filming days in total and I worked out that our caterers must have served in excess of 8,000 lunches!'

Each day's footage or 'rushes' are taken for processing before the careful work of post-production can begin. Editors Ardan Fisher and Derek Bain work alongside the directors to produce a rough cut for initial approval by the team. Each episode goes through several stages of editing, film grading and sound dubbing – including adding on specific bangs for each weapon - to create a finished product ready for transmission on ITV.

Once a 'fine cut' has been done, the assembled episode is shown to *Ultimate Force* composer Rick Wentworth. 'At the beginning the producer and director briefed me on the project and we discussed the sort of house style they were looking for. I read some scripts and put forward various demos that we used to create the title music. Peter Norris told me the music should not be overtly military but have an element of heroism. He wanted something bold but not aggressive. Then I launched myself into the first episode which was quite gruelling. In the opening 90 minutes there are 37 minutes of music, which is a lot. The producer always comes to the "spotting session" when we sit down with the director's fine cut and compare our lists of where we think the music should go. Mostly we cover the same area but he may have technical reasons for adding bits that I hadn't thought of.

Normally TV music cues can be from 30 seconds to three minutes, but on this they are longer.

'*Ultimate Force* has a quasi-orchestral score because television budgets won't allow a full orchestra. I used a basic orchestral group with strings, alto flute, acoustic guitar for lyrical moments and additional percussion where required. It all has to be fairly strident.' Rick mixes the music at his studio in London. 'I record the live instruments at various other studios but the electronics and mixing I do at home. It's a perfect place for directors to meet and discuss the work without the feeling of pressure. About 50 per cent of each music cue for *Ultimate Force* is created technologically – there's so much power within the boxes today. The palette of sounds I have in my studio is enormous.'

Rick began writing music for commercials in the early 1980s, before moving into television and film. His credits include *Withnail and I* and *Cracker*, but he has also worked with Paul McCartney and Roger Waters from Pink Floyd. 'Roger and I have been

Henno's shotgun wounds need a touch more blood between takes.

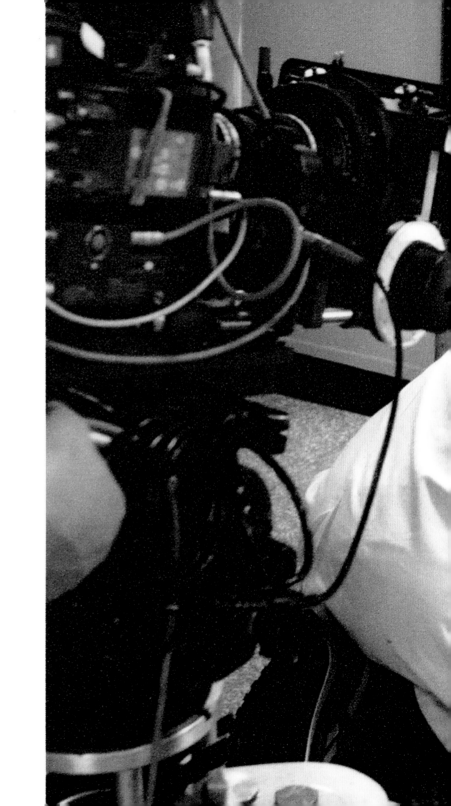

The camera closes in as Caroline tries to save Henno.

working on an opera for a few years, which Paul knew and got in touch. He has made a couple of animated films with me including *The Light Comes From Within* and I did the orchestral arrangement for his Nobel Peace Prize concert in Oslo. I also conducted the music for *Tomb Raider* and *Time Machine* and I'm a professor at the Royal Academy of Music, which is very rewarding.' He adds: 'I don't draw on inspiration for my theme tunes, I just get up in the morning and get on with it – it's more about diligence and perseverance. You have to work hard at it – that's what I tell my students.'

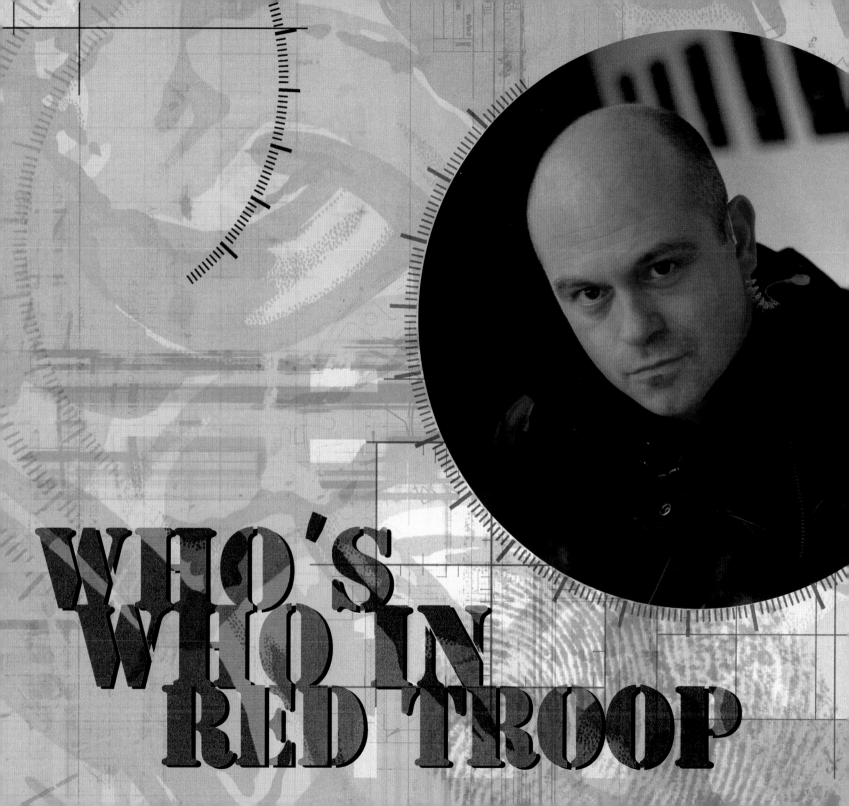

WHO'S WHO IN RED TROOP

Henno Garvie

Full name: Henry William Garvie

Rank: Sergeant

Age: 38

Place of birth:
Frinton-on-Sea, Essex – brought up by his mother with few treats after his father ran off to rejoin the Merchant Navy. As a boy he was taunted mercilessly about the disappearance of his father.

Family:
Lives in Hereford with wife Ruth, whom he married in 1984, and daughters Becky (17) and Lulu (13).

Employment:
After standing up to the bullies, Henno went on to captain the school rugby team and achieved 7 O-levels. In March 1982 he enlisted with the Parachute Regiment where he spent the next seven years. He joined 22 Reg SAS in 1989 and has served for 12 years seeing action in the Gulf, Falklands and Northern Ireland.

Official Assessment:
Intelligent, unflappable, unsentimental, brave and tough as hell.

Danger areas:
The Regiment is his great love. Without it, he could crumble.

22nd REGIMENT FILE

ROSS KEMP PLAYS HENNO GARVIE

Ross Kemp put himself through a rigorous training schedule to develop the stamina and physique of a serving SAS soldier for *Ultimate Force*. 'I like to do something to the best of my ability so I was determined to get very fit to play Henno Garvie. In the weeks before filming I went running around Battersea Park each morning for eight miles. Then I found I had a march fracture in my foot – the sort you get from continuous pounding, so I had to go training with Chris Ryan with a broken foot.'

Ross also spent two months researching the role he describes as the ultimate of dramatic jobs. 'On television we've had everything from firemen to policemen to dustmen. We've had people who work on an oilrig and people on a lifeboat. No-one's tried to tackle the SAS. I can't think of another job that's more dramatic or with more action. The SAS is a secret organization and there is a mystery surrounding them. They are the elite – it's the hardest regiment to get into in the world. These people risk their lives for my country and I applaud that. But they don't tell anyone what they do and they don't expect praise.'

The training weekend with Chris Ryan was the start of a strong working relationship between the actor and the former SAS soldier. Says Ross: 'On the weekend we went marching during the day and at night we had to camp outside. Chris and another SAS guy taught us surveillance and survival – how to camp in the middle of the night, go off and make sure you are not being followed, then come back and find your tent in the dark. They are so highly trained; they could see things we couldn't, like a gamekeeper in his Land Rover waiting for a poacher. At night we slept under a poncho. In the morning Chris came in and asked if we wanted a cup of tea. We all said "that would be lovely" and he just laughed in our faces.

'The SAS talk about life and death in a very easy way. It was great as background material for the characters and we all bonded as a team. Chris is a very interesting character. He was always on hand to advise us and has great charisma. We have become good friends, which I'm really glad about. And he can act as well, dammit!'

Ross's character Sergeant Henno Garvie is the tough but fair leader of Red Troop – a professional soldier who interprets the acronym SAS as 'speed, aggression and surprise'. 'Henno is less talkative and emotional than some of the characters I have played. He is paid to kill people and spends all his time training to do that, which does make him a bit cold-blooded. He has a softer side that he occasionally shows in the way he is protective towards his men, especially Jamie. I am much more emotional than Henno. My father was in the army when I was a child. I wanted to be a soldier but I know I lack the ability to be a soldier in a regiment, which is why I am indebted to the people who protect our lives, our futures and our liberty. The SAS experience life and death at a faster rate than people in civvy street. Having a sense of humour is an essential part of coping with situations they find themselves in, and we've tried very hard to recreate that.'

In the interests of accuracy, Ross learned how to fire weapons, use explosives and stun grenades, and dismantle a gun. 'It's been great running around with guns and fast cars and filming an action adventure series. We couldn't do dangerous stunts but I had a good day in a helicopter where I'm holding a defective soldier out of the door about 900ft off the ground. We are as technically correct

Oblivious to his "wounds", Ross Kemp chats to Chris Ryan.

as you can be in a drama. It's not a documentary and we have to work within budgets and time. The characters have a very busy six weeks but there has to be dramatic licence. We're obviously bending the truth but I don't think we're doing anyone a disservice.'

When he wasn't in front of the camera, Ross enjoyed watching the crew at work. 'I am fascinated by the film production process and I like learning more about the technical side, such as editing or how they produce great special effects on a tight budget. I don't think you can ever learn enough.' Ross had a break from filming when he was invited to 10 Downing Street. 'Cherie Blair rang the producer and asked if I could be released to be Father Christmas at the Barnardo's party at No 10. We were filming that day but I was put on the back of a motorcycle with the red suit and beard flying and was at Downing Street half an hour later. It was worth it just to see the kids' faces.'

Essex-born Ross is one of Britain's favourite actors. He starred as Grant Mitchell in EastEnders for nearly 10 years, leaving to take up an exclusive contract with ITV. His roles have included two series of *Without Motive*, *Hero of the Hour*, *Line in the Sand* and *The Crooked Man*.

Red Troop: the series taught Ross Kemp great respect for real SAS troopers.

Jamie Dow

Full name: James Edward Dow

Rank: Corporal

Age: 24

Place of birth:
Hulme, Greater Manchester

Family:
Father Tommy died in a building-site accident and mother Maureen remarried violent alcoholic Conrad Boyd. Jamie's sister Beth and disabled brother Peter still live at home.

Employment:
Joined the Royal Logistics Corps in 1995 to escape a custodial sentence for stealing cars. Faced with redundancy and in order to combat his fear of physical violence, Jamie tried and passed SAS selection.

Official Assessment:
A crack shot and cool under pressure. With hard work and right grooming could become an ideal trooper.

Danger areas:
Loner with a criminal record for car theft.

22nd REGIMENT FILE

JAMIE DRAVEN PLAYS JAMIE DOW

Jamie Draven describes his experience on *Ultimate Force* as really interesting – even though he was 'tortured'. An episode in the series sees his character Jamie Dow kidnapped by Irish terrorists, taken to a safe house and beaten in an effort to break him down and reveal vital information. Says Jamie: 'It was graphic but there's no way round it. If you're going to do something about torture it has to look right. The lads who played the IRA were all really good. They smacked me about a bit and I got one or two real bumps and bruises.'

Jamie was the first actor approached about starring in *Ultimate Force* and the role appealed immediately. 'Jamie arrives in Red Troop and Henno looks at him and thinks he is someone who can be the best. He tries to guide him through. I was interested in how a young guy from a poor background comes into the SAS. He's trained for a long time and he wants to do his job. But once he gets there, he has to do what he's been trained for, which is killing, with no questions asked. It's interesting how he deals with it, especially as he's got no-one at home to speak to about it. I've never played a soldier before. Everything has to be contained and controlled. You have to hold in your emotions and keep a cool head, especially when you're with everyone else because you've got a job to do.'

Jamie embarked on a programme of fitness training and running to be in top physical condition for the five-month shoot. He also went with the

Jamie received real bumps and bruises during filming.

other actors on the 'outward bound' style weekend organized by Chris Ryan. 'Chris was there with another mate from the SAS and it was good to spend time with them and listen to their stories. It was also great to meet the other lads – they're a fantastic bunch of people and incredible actors. But one night wasn't really enough', he says.

22nd REGIMENT FILE

Alex Leonard

Full name: Alexander Leonard

Rank: Corporal

Age: 27

Place of birth:
Kent

Family:
Fostered then adopted by the Leonard family as a young child, Alex grew up in Canterbury and was educated at the prestigious Kings School. His Asian roots have no relevance to his family.
His brother Sam is also an SAS corporal.

Employment:
Former Air Force officer who resigned his commission to take the gamble of SAS selection. Became friends with Jamie as they experienced selection together before becoming the new recruits to Red Troop.

Official Assessment:
Great sportsman, fine rugby player, horseman and all-round athlete. Rightly proud of his status in the regiment.

Danger areas:
Stiff-upper-lip upbringing may make him unable to cope with tragedy.

'Chris helped us with the gun training as well. He's just a normal guy full of tales, but you've got to think what he did – it's pretty amazing. He's an ordinary bloke, but he did an extraordinary job. When you speak to him about the SAS and what he experienced, I don't know if he blanks it out, but he talks about it like going to the shops and buying a pint of milk. It takes a very special person to be able to do that. They have to get used to it because they're professional soldiers. The reason they're in the SAS is because they're the best of the best.'

As well as firing guns, Jamie also enjoyed the chance to have helicopter rides and drive high-powered cars on a skidpan. 'It was fun – I was really up for all that. It was good to go to work every day, do these things and have a laugh. But I was a bit disappointed we didn't get to do more of our own stunts. When you read a script and you see what's in it you want to do everything that's there.

'Episode one in the Killing House and doing the bank siege was fantastic. We had a lot of time to prepare for that first one and it all comes across well. The blacks we wore are very cool. Everyone wanted to take them home. Even wearing the respirators was amazing because you're in a world of your own. It was nice to wear the gear and feel the part. It's my favourite episode because it's got a lot of heart. I think it's good to show the guys' home lives a bit. I want to know what they do when they go home at the end of the day. Do they switch off or tell the wife and kids how their day's been? Hopefully more of that will come out in the future."

Jamie shot to fame for his role in the smash-hit film *Billy Elliot* and he has also attracted considerable acclaim for his roles in *Butterfly Collectors*, opposite Pete Postlethwaite, and *Messiah*, with Ken Stott.

SENDHIL RAMAMURTHY PLAYS ALEX LEONARD

Sendhil Ramamurthy got some inside knowledge to help him prepare for the role of Alex in *Ultimate Force*. 'A very close friend from drama school knows Sir Peter de la Billière who was colonel of the regiment. He told me loads about it. You can't get it from a better source, so that was a major chunk of my research done. I also got out a video about the training of the SAS.'

Alex Leonard is a new recruit to the SAS when the series begins, joining his brother Sam (Anthony Howell) in Red Troop. 'Alex and Jamie are the young guys of the team and they are inexperienced in some of the SAS ways. They start off as best mates because they've gone through selection together. They are keen and full of bravado. Jamie keeps himself to himself and Alex doesn't own up to any fear, but they have a scene together where they both admit they are scared.

'Alex is adopted; he has been brought into this fairly affluent middle-class family and feels an incredible responsibility to do well. A privileged life seems normal to him but he feels a strong sense of familial loyalty. After things go wrong in the bank siege, he and Jamie clash. Alex is posing as a riot police officer and Jamie is undercover as an anti-

globalist and they have a fight. Alex feels guilty and thinks he should have been there for his brother, but he takes it out on Jamie.'

Playing an SAS trooper had a strong appeal. 'I think anyone would jump at the chance of playing SAS soldiers. The black outfits are just awesome and we loved running around in them because they make you look tough. I didn't know anyone else before we started but I now feel we are best friends for life. When we went on the training days with Chris Ryan and his mate we must have asked 500 questions. They answered in detail and were very physical about it – if it was a question about shooting, they would jump down and do it.

'We had disgusting food, though - dehydrated beef ratatouille, made with hot water heated on portable stoves. It tasted like salty cardboard. We also had chicken soup, which tasted like dirty water. For dessert, we had a fruit dumpling thing. I was the only person who liked that. Then we had pink fish paste with crackers. The tea left much to be desired and we got leaves and branches into it, but we just drank it anyhow. I don't think there was anything left because we had hiked 20kms uphill with heavy rucksacks on and we were starving.'

Sendhil was born in Chicago and lived there and in Texas until the age of 13 when he came to England. 'My parents are both doctors and they wanted to travel for their work. My father is an anaesthetist and now lectures, and my mother is a

Looking the part, but Sendhil Ramamurthy was unimpressed by dehydrated SAS rations.

leading neonatal expert in the States. My sister Sujatha followed them and she's in her third year of medical school.'

Sendhil took a different direction, training in drama at the Webber Douglas Academy, where he met his wife, Polish-born actress Olga Sosnovska. 'We've been married for three years and we've both been working constantly, which means we have been apart. But we never stay away from each other for too long. Olga was in Turkey for *Jason and the Argonauts* and I flew out to see her, and when I was in Budapest for Hallmark's *In The Beginning* she came out there. We are always travelling and have a place in Manhattan that is a second home.'

Travelling is something Sendhil and his character share. 'As a child I was nomadic and, like Alex I enjoy travel as part of my career. I had a privileged upbringing too, but the similarities stop there. He is a very broody character, which I don't think I am. And in real life I would never want to be in the SAS shooting guns, but I do enjoy playing at it.'

TONY CURRAN PLAYS PETE TWAMLEY

Tony Curran describes SAS soldier Pete Twamley as a tough cookie with a sensitive side. 'Twamley has been in the regiment for about 12 years and he's been married for the same time. He's committed to both. He is quite a hard man but he's also the loyal, supportive one of the team – if he gets aggressive there is a reason for it. He's been a bit wild in the past

Pete Twamley

Full name: Peter Twamley

Rank: Corporal

Age: 36

Place of birth:
Glasgow, the only boy of six children.

Family:
Happily married to his childhood sweetheart and a loving
father to Robbie (8) and Heather (6). Mrs Twamley is the
only wife readily accepted among the troop.

Employment:
A former cadet, he was accepted into the Black Watch in
1984 before joining the Royal Engineers where he was
assigned to 321 Explosive Ordinance Disposal. He passed
SAS selection at first attempt and has been stationed at
Hereford for the past 12 years.

Official Assessment:
Father of the team, unflinchingly loyal to Henno.
Always ready to offer advice but only when asked.

Danger areas:
Loves his wife and wants to be there for his children.
Can snap when pushed too far.

22nd REGIMENT FILE

and he, Henno and Ricky have been through a lot together. He's grown up now and he's got a sensible head on young shoulders. He does have a sensitive side – when he shoots someone he has a tendency to be sick afterwards. It's his way of dealing with it.

'Pete Twamley doesn't bend, he snaps. He snaps at his kids when he is packing in episode six – it comes from his frustration at having to leave and fearing that he might not be coming back. All these characters have dark sides. As SAS soldiers they have to dehumanize. Their responsibility is astonishing. There is a scene where Twamley realizes he may have to blow himself up. Like motorcycle couriers, they have to be a bit mad to do the job but there is method to the madness. It's a vocation and the dedication runs through them.'

Twamley's dedication is something Tony shares. 'I like him as a character, he has a good sense of humour. I am dedicated as an actor and as a person. He gets focused and so do I – we are both committed to the cause, whatever that happens to be. But I am not married and don't have kids, so I took that part of him from the script.

'It really helped to get into character when we had the gear on. Wearing the black combats and carrying the MP5 makes you feel like the ultimate soldier. And after playing the role, I found I was acting a bit more responsibly.' Like the others, Tony found the involvement of Chris Ryan and the other specialists invaluable. 'On the training weekend, Chris made us run through the forest late at night and he was shouting at us to run, saying the farmer might be trying to shoot us. I was running really fast

Man in black: Tony Curran felt like the ultimate soldier.

and my heart was beating faster. I felt powerful and professional at the same time and I tried to remember that when we were filming.

22nd REGIMENT FILE

Ricky Mann

Full name: Richard Mann

Rank: Corporal

Age: 30

Place of birth:
London

Family:
Married to a woman who still lives in East Timor and dreams of settling down on a farm with her when his time is served.

Employment:
First black Sergeant in the Irish Guards, but when pressed for details of his life prior to the army the shutters come down.

Official Assessment:
Easy going and warm but possesses the coldness of the best contract killer when required. A good survivor and a chameleon who is expert at adopting different personas.

Danger areas:
Can be a daredevil and occasionally morose when he misses his wife.

'In episode six I have to show a group of men how to dismantle an AK47, which was quite hard to work with. The armourer helped me and I picked it up easily. I practised firing and spent an hour and a half taking it apart. By the time we came to film it had become like another limb.

'Henno and Twamley are in a deserted field training soldiers. We double-cross the soldiers and I fire 30 to 40 rounds of bullets above their heads. I did that about four times for different camera angles. *Ultimate Force* was the first time I had fired weapons and it does give you a rush of adrenaline. I don't really like guns but it felt real. We didn't want to try to act like tough guys, we wanted to look like the real thing – soldiers who also have a bit of a laugh. Those relationships spilled over into real life and we all got on really well. After the wrap party, I watched Celtic win the league and then went skiing for a week with Elliot Cowan.'

Tony is from Glasgow, where he studied at the RSC before moving to London in the mid-1990s. His credits include the feature films *Blade 2* with Wesley Snipes, *Gladiator*, *Pearl Harbor*, *Shallow Grave*, and *The 13th Warrior* with Antonio Banderas. On television, Tony has appeared in *Perfect World*, *Undercover Heart*, *Mists of Avalon*, *Shockers II* and *Touching Evil*.

'I get most recognized from *This Life* where I played Ferdy's boyfriend Lenny. I had long curly hair and Lenny was quite bohemian and avant-garde. My Celtic looks have helped me. I got a lot of parts through my long red hair. I had it for three or four years and wore it in a ponytail. But it took a lot of looking after and I can't imagine going back to it

now.' Tony's hair was cut for *Menace* on Channel 5 where he plays a hardnosed cop called DC Skinner. He also plays a spy, Rodney Skinner, in a new film called *The League of Extraordinary Gentlemen*, which is filming in Iceland, Venice and Prague and stars Sean Connery.

DANNY SAPANI PLAYS RICKY MANN

Ricky Mann is a combination of Jonah Lomu and 'The Thing' from *Marvel* comics, according to Danny Sapani who plays him. 'He's a big guy with a big heart. A reliable warrior and a romantic. When I was a kid I always wanted to be The Thing – a big guy who could turn into anything and save people. That's what Ricky is in *Ultimate Force* – I finally got my dream!

'Ricky is very confident with a dry sense of humour. He is the demolition man – the Jonah Lomu of the team. He has the SAS stare, the very black and white view of death, but he's the most sorted of them all. He's the mainstay of Red Troop and if he was to crack up, they'd be in trouble. He and Henno have an understanding and trust that goes way back. Henno won't show emotion to many people but Ricky knows him and loves him like a brother. Ricky appears to be second in command tacitly and doesn't question that. He doesn't have to prove anything and he's not striving to knock anyone off his perch.'

Ricky and Danny share some similarities. 'He's not ambitious which makes him the very opposite of me. But what we do share is the love of what we do. My dedication to my craft and the passion and pleasure of work – that is our main similarity. Ricky is married to a girl in East Timor and he misses her. I find his love and commitment inspiring and I love his sense of humour too. I am a bit like that, when I am on form, and I've got a big heart too. When I get the balance right between maudlin and aggressive I can be quite sharp and dry. But I'm not sure I've got the moral flexibility you need to pass the test for the SAS. I can understand it and see it in people but I'm not sure I can see it in myself. I like to think I can stand up to things but the killing doesn't settle easily with me. I think it must be hard to keep a relationship going unless you were involved with someone in the same regiment. It would be good to explore more of their personal lives in another series, although part of their appeal is their anonymity and their love and commitment for the SAS above all.'

Danny enjoyed scenes demonstrating Ricky's love of food. 'In episode one, Ricky cooks an amazing meal when the troop are sent off to a hotel. You think he has gone off to get a few steaks and he comes back with this huge cow. It took two people to get the slab of meat on my shoulders. I am a pretty strong guy, but it was heavy. It was great fun to do, but the meat we cooked up was inedible because it was really for braising, although it looked good on camera. We had one slab that was fried for Jamie to taste and we all had a bit of that. I have to admit, the last thing I could think of eating that night when I got home was steak!

'The scene showed what the SAS are like in a humorous way. They are intelligent and cultured people; they can adapt to any situation and know about wine. They don't do anything by halves, hence the grand table set for dinner, the cut glass and grapes hanging from jars – it ends up being a sumptuous banquet. The design department did a great job and it makes me out to be a superhero. There's no way I could do that on my own. I like cooking but my partner who's from Thailand is a fantastic cook.'

Cooking a banquet was easy compared with learning one particular line of dialogue. 'In episode two I just have to get out of a car and give the registration number of another car in police oscar bravo style. I found it really difficult; I think it was a case of having to learn lots of information very quickly. It was funny but we got there in the end.'

Before working on *Ultimate Force*, Danny played a soldier in the play *To The Green Fields Beyond* at the Donmar Warehouse, directed by Sam Mendes and starring Ray Winstone. His other credits include *Holby City*, *Trial and Retribution* and *Between The Lines*.

Born in London of Ghanaian descent, Danny and his partner have a six-year-old daughter Saeng-fah and a one-year-old son Blu. 'I love being a dad and one of the good things about being an actor is that you can be around a lot for the children and help look after them. Although we're based in London, we have a house in Bangkok. I would love to live for six months of the year in Thailand.'

ELLIOT COWAN PLAYS JEM POYNTON

Elliot Cowan trained for his role in *Ultimate Force* by doing salsa dancing. 'Salsa is great because you come out sweating and aching but it is a stylish and ostentatious way of keeping fit. I thought it was quite relevant for the part of Jem. For someone like him it could be another credential to use with women.

'Jem is a womanizing, wisecracking, self-centred joker who needs to be in the centre of attention. I wanted to play the role because he is a charismatic man who's proud of being in the SAS and uses it to his advantage. He dolls himself up more than the other lads and has a collection of sunglasses – Oakley wraparounds for jogging, tortoiseshell Raybans in his civvies and Aviators to go with his blacks. He's pretty vain but he's a bright bloke too – bilingual and picks up new skills fast. Jem has worked hard in the military and quickly rose to fame in the SAS. He's young and ambitious and wants to make the best of what comes his way. He relies on quick-thinking and jokes to get what he wants. But he is ultimately insecure about being usurped by young blood like Jamie coming in.'

Elliot likes his character – up to a point. 'I would go out for a drink with Jem but he would drop you once he met a woman and you'd never be guaranteed a spare bed at his place. But up to that time you would have a good laugh. I didn't want to make him some blond brawny bimbo – I wanted him to have humour and intelligence. He is very happy in his own body. I'm pretty fit like him, but he is more brutal than I am. He has a past that is unsalubrious – he hasn't always operated on the right side of the tracks. His hard outer shell hides insecurity deep down.'

Elliot was delighted to win the role of Jem only months after leaving RADA – but his first meeting with the rest of the cast didn't go entirely to plan. 'We were all going off training with Chris Ryan, but I'd been out late the night before, slept through my alarm and missed my car. So I had to set off to find the farm on my own and got a speeding ticket and a burst tyre. I turned up with a beard and long hair and expected to be shunned by all the other actors. But they took me under their wing and looked after me.

'Chris shouted at us in the middle of the night, made up pitch camp at 1am then kicked us up a hill – and it was quite unifying for us all! Since then we have formed genuine friendships. We take risks in front of the camera because we know we can.' Chris Ryan also helped Elliot practise his skills with a gun. 'Jem is a sniper, as Chris was when he was in the SAS. There were techniques that I wanted to learn to get it right. Even holding the rifle in a certain way makes it look as if you've been holding it for years. There were strange forms you could adopt to give yourself a natural, confident look.

'Snipers consider themselves technical experts. Jem is never quite given the opportunity to use his skills because of Jamie, but he has to keep up to scratch. Chris's expertise was also useful when I have an unarmed combat scene in episode three. It was choreographed by the stuntman Colin Skeaping and was really good and physical. In episode two I

TOP SECRET

Jem Poynton

Full name: Jeremy Poynton

Rank: Corporal

Age: 28

Family:
The result of a loveless marriage between a former Brigadier and a trophy wife 25 years his junior, Jem went to boarding school where he failed his A-levels due to smoking too much dope.

Employment:
Joined the Green Howards as a private in 1990. With the 'travelling regiment' he took part in adventurous training expeditions to Pakistan, South Georgia, Spain and Canada. Passed selection into 22 Reg in 1997.

Official Assessment:
Natural athlete and excellent sniper. Good at undercover work and at killing.

Danger areas:
A glory hunter with a fragile ego and a tendency to jealousy. Likes fast cars, designer clothes and women. Remains incapable of maintaining a serious relationship with anyone but himself.

22nd REGIMENT FILE

had to vault a wooden fence in a back garden. I worked with Colin again and after a few practices got it down to a fine art. But on the actual take the adrenaline started flowing, things came unstuck and I brought down some of the fence.

'In many of the episodes we have to climb on the top of buildings, over roofs and down skylights. The Killing House scene involved a lot of running, in and out of buildings, and you get a sense of how strenuous it can be for the real SAS. Carrying the kit, you have to kick down the doors, the adrenaline makes your heart beat faster, the gas mask limits your vision and breathing so you genuinely get a sense of what it must be like. Being a young and athletic actor, I take it all in my stride!'

Since leaving drama school, Elliot has appeared in *Rescue Me*, *Jonathan Creek*, *The Blooding* and *Crims*. 'I've found my casting has contrasted from one end of the spectrum to the other. I have played soldiers before and also cerebral people, along the angelic line. I get cast as characters who have a darker element to them, perhaps in contrast to my looks. It's great to be a young actor on the front line of a new series. It's a great learning curve and I've met actors who have become mates. We had a laugh filming the opening titles because we were asked to look tough and smouldering, but we ended up singing 'Blue Velvet', although you don't hear it because they are just visual sequences with the title music played over. So as we walk up the airstrip after a hard day's battle we're all singing. It didn't sound too bad either, but you'll never get to hear that.'

Jem (Elliot Cowan) has a pair of sunglasses for every occasion.

Caroline Walshe

Full name: Caroline Walshe

Rank: Captain

Age: 27

Place of birth:
Reigate, Surrey

Family:
The daughter of an Anglican minister and a comprehensive schoolteacher, Caroline was a high achiever at school. She is single and determined to stay that way - her career comes first.

Employment:
Went to Sandhurst in 1993 - one of very few accepted without a degree. Made a junior commander with the Combat Support Arms Intelligence Corps, serving in Africa, Northern Ireland and Kuwait. She reached the rank of Captain early at 25, and also obtained her degree in Computer Sciences. Posted to the Regiment in 2001.

Official Assessment:
A skilled interrogator, communications expert and man-manager. Also a tomboy who is determined to show a woman can match a man in the toughest of their backyards.

Danger areas:
Her desire to be at the sharp end - especially if she is injured - could have a disruptive influence on the men of Red Troop.

ALEX REID PLAYS CAPTAIN CAROLINE WALSHE

Alex Reid jumped at the chance to play a woman in a man's world in *Ultimate Force* – once she knew her character was more than a token female. 'The books written about the SAS don't really mention any women so I asked if it was right that there would be female officers in the regiment. The answer is that they are assigned to the SAS and often used for undercover work. So Caroline is quite legitimate. She's an intelligence officer on attachment. She's not at all flaky – she'd never survive if she was. She's completely used to the banter and the digs she gets and she's OK with it. She's not cold but she's ambitious, strong and determined and knows what she is letting herself in for by going into that male-dominated world.'

Caroline is keen to get a slice of the action. 'No matter what job she was in, she would want to work her way up and do well. In the SAS she wants to get involved wherever it's feasibly possible. There are restrictions on how far you can go as a woman, for example, you would never have a female storming a bank in the blacks, but Caroline stretches those boundaries as far as she can', says Alex. 'She is trained in using arms but has conversations with Henno when she tells him she feels like a tea lady. She says "I can do more, please use me", and gradually he does. She goes undercover and she gets shot. By episode five and six she is regarded as one of the team.

Caroline (Alex Reid) frequently puts her career before affairs of the heart.

'I enjoyed the action a lot. I trained beforehand by going to the gym, eating healthily and getting a lot of sleep but as the series went on there was more and

22nd REGIMENT FILE

Dotsy Doheny

Full name: Dennis Doheny

Rank: Lieutenant

Age: 28

Place of birth:
Salcombe, Devon

Family:
Dotsy grew up in Seaview, Isle of Wight, in a privileged army family.

Employment:
Educated at Eton, Cambridge and Sandhurst before joining the Guards. Went through SAS selection to become Commander of Red Troop after only six months.

Official Assessment:
Did well on selection and has the makings of a good Troop
Commander. Keen to prove himself and win the respect of the men.

Danger areas:
Inexperienced - needs to watch his decision-making when under pressure. Needs to establish his authority among more experienced troopers.

more action so just going to work was enough. I was able to do all the action sequences myself – it was rolls on the floor and diving. At one point Caroline gets shot, which was really interesting. I had a blood sac on my body and the timing of the gunshot, my reaction and setting off the squibs to burst the blood sac was very strange and technical. But it all comes together well.'

Before she is shot, Caroline herself fires her gun at a terrorist. 'I went on weapons training with the armourer, Tack, and apparently I wasn't too bad a shot. We used real bullets and the kickback you get from even a small handgun is something you have to get used to. I was quite conscious of how I held the gun, too. But I didn't let the side down. If there was a scene one day where I was using a gun, Tack would take me to practise at lunchtime and make sure I knew what I was doing. I'm OK about using guns in a drama, as long as it's controlled and you have a respect for the guns and the people you're working with. We were able to practise, knew the roles and the armourers always made sure the barrels were clear. It was so well co-ordinated that I felt quite safe.'

Aside from work, Caroline becomes the object of attention from some of the members of Red Troop. 'She has to keep her distance. Within that environment you have to be very careful about forming any sort of relationship. It's not allowed, although I'm sure it still goes on. For her to achieve her ambitions, she has to maintain her professionalism. So she copes with it by giving as good as she gets', says Alex. 'The job wouldn't appeal to me because there is a lot of sexism in the army. I can completely relate to the desire to prove yourself but don't know if on a daily basis I could hold my tongue enough, which she seems to do quite well. I imagine it must be very frustrating.'

In real life Alex quickly became one of the 'boys'. 'I didn't really think about being the only woman but luckily they are a lovely bunch of lads. Whenever I needed to escape from an all-male environment I went to the make-up truck for a natter. And at the end I bought the guys some water pistols because I thought they'd all miss their guns! They were spraying them around when they were in their make-up and costumes but no-one seemed to mind because it was the last week of filming.'

Alex comes from Cornwall and trained at the Webber Douglas Academy. Her other credits include the lead role of Nell Brennan in *Blue Dove*, *Relic Hunter*, *As If* and the films *Last Orders* and *Arachnid*.

JAMIE BAMBER PLAYS LT DOTSY DOHENY

Jamie Bamber didn't get to fire a gun until the last week of filming *Ultimate Force*. 'My character Dotsy Doheny is an officer so he doesn't get much action until episode six. He desperately wants to show the men that he is hands-on and prove he's one of the team. But my boots were always pristine and parade shiny. Both on and off the set the boys were always taking the mickey about how I didn't get dirty. I got so much grief for not firing a gun, either. So at the

Jamie Bamber felt he lost his virginity as a soldier when he fired a gun in episode 6.

end when he finally gets the camouflage make-up on, goes into the bushes and uses a gun it was great. I felt as if I'd lost my virginity as a soldier!'

Jamie enjoyed portraying Dotsy's dilemma in his role as a 'Rupert'. 'Dotsy has a family history of serving in the armed forces. He went to Eton, Cambridge, Sandhurst and then into the Guards which is a prestigious regiment. But he is someone who has to prove himself above and beyond the traditional approach. Going into the SAS is not a soft option and he had to go through the same training and selection as the men.

'He is saddled with being in charge from day one – that is the crux of his whole character. He has to deal with these superior troopers who have field experience of many years. He has been given authority by the army but personally and practically he is inferior to these men. It's a diplomatic path he has to tread. As soon as you meet him, his authority is undermined straightaway. Henno says "never ever call a Rupert sir" and this becomes a running gag throughout the series. He has only been there for six months so he fulfils every preconceived idea that they have of a young officer and they dismiss him as another chinless wonder. But he is tough enough from the training and has genuine qualities. And the men do eventually warm to him.'

Ultimate Force is not the first time Jamie has been in uniform. 'I was an American soldier in *Band of Brothers* and I played Kennedy, the right hand man, in *Hornblower*, but I've never worn contemporary combats before. Putting the boots and the trousers on makes you feel very military. When I wore the beret for the first time I was besieged by everyone about how to wear it. Chris Ryan put it under water, shrank it a bit, took out a pocket razor and shaved the fluff off and shaped it on my head. There was a constant battle with wardrobe who wanted to raise it so the camera could see my face, while Chris wanted it tight on my eyebrows.'

Jamie kept ultra-fit during filming by training for the 2002 London Marathon. He went on to complete the race in less than three hours, raising money for leukaemia research. 'I love scuba diving, skiing, tennis and golf, but running is my main sport. I trained for the marathon all the way through filming *Ultimate Force*. It was tough but it kept me fit. Every muscle aches when you're running that sort of distance and I won't miss the blisters. It was a great adrenaline high but I'm not sure if I could do it again.'

Jamie was born in London to an Irish mother and American father and lived in Paris as a child. He studied Italian and French at Cambridge before going to LAMDA.

Since leaving drama school, Jamie has appeared in *The Scarlet Pimpernel*, *Poirot*, *Lady Audley's Secret*, *Bob Martin* and the role of Matthew Kendal in *Peak Practice*. He also starred in the feature film *Shifting Sands*.

MILES ANDERSON PLAYS COLONEL AIDAN DEMPSEY

Miles Anderson has impeccable credentials for playing an SAS colonel – his father formed the Rhodesian SAS and his elder brother was a Brigadier in the British army. 'I was destined to be in the army because all I remember as a kid was living in an army family. My father was a major general and formed C Squadron which in those days was a Rhodesian SAS. He tried to oppose Ian Smith and we had to leave the country. My eldest brother had joined the Rhodesian army as a cadet then went to Sandhurst and joined the 6th Ghurkas and commanded them. He ended up as a Brigadier and my younger brother was a 6th Ghurka as well.

'I got into the army by default, first playing a Colonel in *Soldier Soldier* and now Dempsey in *Ultimate Force*. Dempsey is very close to my brother. Tough, uncompromising, erudite and charming – a man who lives, eats and sleeps the army. He's much harder than the character I played in *Soldier Soldier*. Dempsey would be quite happy shooting someone in the back of the head, although he's got a very soft spot for the blokes he commands. The priority is always the men and the men's safety – everything else comes second.'

Miles' upbringing meant the weapons in *Ultimate Force* were nothing new. 'I grew up with weapons. There were three brothers in the family and at 12 years old we were each issued with 12-bores. But unfortunately I don't get involved in much action. Dempsey never puts on the backpack or shoots the gun; he sits in the office directing operations and decides which troop gets the gig. I would describe him as an upmarket fixer. When there is an operation that is highly sensitive he's there. It's an old boy network – he has friends in the MOD and

Aidan Dempsey

Full name: Aidan Dempsey

Rank: Colonel

Age: 48

Place of birth:
Rhodesia, now Zimbabwe. Dempsey was an only child who grew up on his parents' ranch.

Family:
His father was a senior civil servant in the British Consulate before taking up a post as Director of MI5. Dempsey was a boarder at Wellington school from the age of 13 and studied History and Latin at Trinity College, Dublin. Married to Kate and the father of three boys.

Employment:
Dempsey underwent officer training as an Artillery Commander before serving with the 32nd Reg Royal Artillery. He was awarded the Military Cross after the Falklands War. He served as General de la Billière's number two in the Gulf and led the British Forces advance on to Iraqi soil in Desert Storm. On his return to the UK, Dempsey was promoted to Lieutenant Colonel and put in command of 22nd Regiment in Hereford.

Official Assessment:
Very experienced and reliable. The welfare of his men comes first.

Danger areas:
Wants to get involved in the heart of the action, not always behind-the-scenes.

22nd REGIMENT FILE

Destiny calls: Miles Anderson follows family tradition by joining Ultimate Force's *SAS.*

foreign office and the military attachés always know him. I've met a couple of SAS commanding officers and they are off the wall. One wore an immaculate Savile Row suit with battered desert boots. I think you have to be eccentric to be in that game.

'I've been very close to the army all my life so I know how true to life the series is. Rob Heyland writes good, three-dimensional characters and the moment I saw it, I knew that I wanted it. It's very close to the real thing and that's the advantage of

Mick Sharp

Full name: Michael Sharp

Rank: Sergeant, Parachute Regiment

Age: 23

Place of birth:
London

Family:
Adopted as a child and grew up on a housing estate in south London. All attempts to find his birth mother and father have failed.

Employment:
A good soldier, reaching the rank of sergeant in the Paras. Tried for SAS selection with Jamie Dow but failed at his first attempt. Mick has only one more chance to make it.

Official Assessment:
Determined to make the grade but still has a long way to go.

Danger areas:
Sensitive about his family background and has a fear of water.

22nd REGIMENT FILE

having Chris Ryan as adviser.'

Miles' credits include *Family Affairs*, *Have Your Cake And Eat It*, *Into the Blue* and *The Rector's Wife*. He returned to his home country, now Zimbabwe, in 1986 to shoot the film *Cry Freedom*, and went back again, after completing work on *Ultimate Force*, to witness the country's general election. 'I decided to follow my heart and be in my country during its greatest hour. It was an amazing experience to be there at such a momentous time – it was moving, frightening and ultimately depressing. At times it was so scary it was a bit like an SAS mission. I just wish I'd had the team with me.'

Miles' own life couldn't be more different from that of an SAS colonel. He and his wife, casting agent Lesley Duff, live in a houseboat near Hampton Court. 'We built it from scratch and it was designed by Royal naval architect John Heath who did the boats for *Hornblower* and some Bond films. It looks like a cartoon boat; it's bright yellow and 3,000 square feet in size, complete with four bathrooms. It was a moment of madness to do it, but Lesley and I feel it is one of the best life changes we have made.'

LAURENCE FOX PLAYS MICK SHARP

Laurence Fox spent 12 hours in a freezing cold river in February – all for the love of playing SAS wannabe Mick Sharp. 'The episode "Natural Selection" is all about the recruiting process and the episode spins around Mick's attempts to get through. We had to cross a swollen river all day. I got into it at first but by about half past seven at night I couldn't take it any more. Even though I had a dry suit on, I am fairly scrawny and it doesn't really protect you from the cold. I earned my money that day – I hope it was worth it!

'I had to wear old World War II battledress and run through the woods. Obviously we are actors so we got a better deal than the real SAS, who have to strip off to go across the river. I had space blankets and make-up people being nice to me with cups of tea. And after we were hauled out we had a hot Jacuzzi which was heavenly warm.'

Laurence enjoys tennis and water-skiing, which helped him prepare for the role. 'You have to be fairly fit and pretend to be the hardest blokes on earth if you're in the SAS. Mates of mine are in the regular army and they think it's amusing that I am playing a soldier. I was in the combined cadet force at school – little did I know that my early training would come in useful!

'In another scene I have to drive a huge truck called a Unimog – a huge thing with tyres as big as me. They made me drive it at the last minute then lumber out of it with a massive machine gun. It was great fun getting to shoot all the guns. The cast are a bunch of great guys; they welcomed me in. I took great pleasure in winding up Chris Ryan and trying to beat him up. I am sure he was scared of me, although he hid it well.'

Mick is desperate to make it into the SAS and join his mate Jamie Dow (Jamie Draven). Laurence

Sam (Anthony Howell) is in the firing line when things go wrong. Right: Dressed in black combats and respirators, SAS troopers are anonymous killers, identified only by numbers on their jackets.

other. Mick is known for his malapropisms. He gets phrases wrong but he doesn't realise he is doing it and can't see what's funny. I have to admit I didn't get the jokes sometimes either so perhaps it is perfect casting. Superficially we share some characteristics but we are actually very different. Mick had a tough life, he was brought up on a council estate, which is not similar to anything I have known.'

Laurence is the son of actor James Fox and was educated at Harrow before studying drama at RADA. 'I wanted to go to university but I couldn't get in, so I went to Africa driving safaris for six months, then worked as a landscape gardener and then went to the Royal Academy. I knew I wanted to be an actor from early on but I didn't want to attempt it until I'd got through school. Although I come from an acting family we don't really talk about it, although I might ask my father's advice every now and again.' *Ultimate Force* is Laurence's first TV role – but at the age of 23 he is already a veteran of feature films including the Oscar-winning *Gosford Park*, which he filmed in his third year at drama school, and *The Hole*, filmed in his second year. His other film work includes *Deathwatch* with Jamie Bell, and *South of Grenada*.

explains: 'He didn't make it through selection the first time so this is his last chance. Like a lot of soldiers who haven't fired many rounds of bullets, he is nervous of shooting or killing anyone. But he and Jamie have a mutual deal; they look out for each

ANTHONY HOWELL PLAYS SAM LEONARD

Playing a soldier is second nature to Anthony Howell. As well as his role as Sam in *Ultimate Force*, he also plays an invalided wartime soldier in *Foyle's War*. 'It's strange to get two roles as a soldier but

they are very different. *Foyle's War* is set in World War II so it was good to do a contemporary piece like *Ultimate Force*.

'Sam is an ex-public school boy who went into the army and decided to try for the SAS, which isn't uncommon. It's a hard job – if you are ambitious in terms of climbing the career ladder you probably wouldn't do it. He is officer material and his contemporaries would have gone up to major in the same time. But he chose the SAS because he has a strong sense of justice, of what is right and wrong. He has been brought up in a very well-off family, but they are socially aware and responsible, too. Sam is stoical and a good man. He hasn't just hung around the playing fields of Eton.'

Sam is proud when his brother Alex (Sendhil Ramamurthy) joins Red Troop. 'Sam's parents adopted Alex when he was a baby. They have grown up together and have a strong bond. Although Sam is protective, they are both aware that they have to keep their own identities. Alex wouldn't push his luck and expect big brother to get him out of a scrape. But if there was real danger, Sam would be there.'

Anthony enjoyed taking part in the two-day training course with Chris Ryan. 'It was invaluable. We learned so much. Just reading around the subject is not enough to get into their heads. They are incredible men and after the second day I had such respect for them. I think they are superhuman – we can only hope to portray that accurately.'

Anthony trained at the Drama Centre and spent a year with the Royal Shakespeare Company. His other TV roles include *Helen West* with Amanda Burton, *Swallow* and *Wives and Daughters*. He stars as Paul Milner in *Foyle's War* alongside Michael Kitchen. 'The difference between Sam Leonard and Milner is that Milner is required to kill for his country in the war but it's not part of his real make-up. Sam has chosen to join the SAS of his own free will – and accepts that he will kill as part of his job.'

THE STORY SO FAR

EPISODE 1 : THE KILLING HOUSE

Jamie Dow and Alex Leonard are the new recruits to Red Troop. There is no such thing as a gentle introduction to the SAS, however, and the new boys are tied up and put straight into a hostage-rescue exercise in the Killing House. Nervous, yet excited, they are liberated by troopers using live ammunition.

Afterwards, the new boys meet their leader – tough, determined and professional soldier Henno Garvie. Both impress him – Jamie with his shy resilience and Alex with his eager enthusiasm. But both soldiers have a lot to learn – for a start, they have never killed. Alex's brother Sam, the huge and affable Ricky Mann, the attractive but vain Jem Poynton, and the good-natured old hand Pete Twamley make up the rest of the team.

Armed with his black SAS uniform, an HK MP5 machine gun and a Sig Sauer pistol, Jamie wants another go in the Killing House – but this time on the other side of the doors. With live firing, this is an exercise of life or death. Henno warns the recruits to prepare for killing so they don't freeze. And he warns that any team member who gets hit must be left where he lies. Any hesitation and another could fall.

As they run the high-risk exercise again and again, Duggan, an armed robber, assembles a team for a raid on a bank to steal Euros. He names his

Jamie runs from the helicopter to join Alex on their first operation.

chosen gang Pug, Badger, Weasel and Lofty and issues them with pistols and two pump shotguns. Badger has never killed, but he gets no chance to practise. His only drill is to drive the getaway car.

Practicising on the skid pan at Hereford, Jamie is surprised to find his sister Beth watching him. She tells him their mother has suffered a stroke. To the disbelief of Henno, troop commander Dotsy Doheny gives permission for Jamie to take leave. Jamie goes but has no real desire to return to his roots or see his violent step-father.

Duggan's raid runs according to plan, until a policeman taps on the window of Badger's car. He is parked on double yellow lines. Startled, the young man's nerves fail. The policeman asks him to get out and his pistol falls to the ground. A woman calls 999 and Badger pushes the cop into the bank to the wailing sound of approaching squad cars. The burglary has escalated into a hostage situation.

The SAS are put on standby. Henno's men are ready and he wins the job for his team against fellow sergeant Johnny Bell, leader of Blue Troop. A helicopter goes to pick up Jamie to the amazement of his family.

From an operations room at a local school, the police attempt negotiations with Duggan. Henno is sceptical about the likelihood of the gang surrendering, and mobilizes Red Troop to prepare for an attack, with the help of a modeller, an architect and a security systems expert. Red Troop spends the night at a local hotel, where Ricky Mann cooks and serves an enormous banquet. Alex and Jamie can't sleep, nervous at the thought of their first big operation.

By the next morning tension is escalating in the bank. SAS intelligence officer, Captain Caroline Walshe, has identified Duggan as a disgraced Flying Squad officer, discharged for unlawful killing. Enraged when promised transport fails to arrive, Duggan shoots Badger without hesitation. The body is dumped outside the bank and the police relinquish control to the SAS.

Equipped with MP5s, explosives and stun grenades, Red Troop storm the bank in a tremendous show of firepower. But as Jamie and Alex face the adrenaline rush of their first real SAS operation, they discover that the life or death exercises become dramatically and tragically real…

EPISODE 2 : JUST A TARGET

As Red Troop prepare to bury Sam Leonard with full military honours in the churchyard at Hereford, a lone gunman attempts to assassinate a prominent European banker at a French chateau. Due to his inexperience, however, the gunman misses his target and the banker, Lunberg, is able to flee.

At the barracks, Jamie meets Sam's mother. He feels awkward and is grateful when Henno comes to his rescue. Henno betrays no emotion, dealing professionally and courteously with Sam's parents – but when they have left the wake, he lets his guard down and uncharacteristically has too much to drink. A sober Jamie gets him home.

At base the following morning, a senior MI5 official briefs the team on the assassination

A grieving Alex supports his mother at Sam's funeral.

attempt. Chillingly, Henno realises the gun was an awesomely powerful sniper's rifle, never yet used on mainland Britain. It must be found urgently – another hit and lives could be lost.

MI5 suspect the rifle and the shooter are now in the UK with an anti-capitalist group thought to be behind the shooting. An MI5 mole has already infiltrated the faction and the intelligence service wants an SAS trooper to join her. Jamie is an excellent sniper and Henno puts him forward.

With the help of MI5 undercover operative Lorraine, Jamie is introduced to the group. He poses as her boyfriend, Tony, an ex-soldier with sniper experience. He's invited to attend a rally, which soon disintegrates into violence.

At the heart of the riot, police set upon one group member, Flossie. Jamie wades in to help her and is brutally attacked. The fight is a set up, however, with Henno and Red Troop acting the part of the riot police so that Jamie can save Flossie and make himself the hero of the day.

Red Troop bug the group's headquarters but their search reveals no sign of the rifle. It seems the anti-globalists intend to strike again but the target and location of the hit are unknown. Box 500 (intelligence officer) hacks into Flossie's computer as the SAS play a waiting game.

Lorraine is becoming unstable and Jamie fears she will jeopardise his mission. There is a major breakthrough, though, when Jamie befriends Simon. The young radical is in awe of him, admitting he probably couldn't kill anyone. Simon even suggests he was the mysterious shooter. Jamie seizes the opportunity and gets Simon to believe he would be willing to take his place in another assassination attempt.

Troubled since the death of Sam, Henno visits Caroline late at night, but they end up simply talking. Meanwhile Jamie is chosen as the new assassin, but MI5 still have no idea where the hit is going to take place. Henno realises it is time to take matters into their own hands.

Suddenly Flossie bursts in on Jamie, telling him it is time to go. Jamie rushes from the house, forgetting the tracking device hidden in his belt, while Lorraine unwittingly lets slip his real name. Red Troop attempt to keep him under surveillance but Jamie is ordered to switch cars.

He is taken to a deserted quarry when he finally gets his hands on the gun. But as he zeroes the dangerous rifle, he is told the anti-capitalists will kill Lorraine if he does not do as he is told. With the clock ticking, Red Troop must track down both Jamie and Lorraine – and locate Lunberg – before Jamie is forced to complete the anti-capitalists' deadly work.

EPISODE 3 : NATURAL SELECTION

Two hundred hopeful recruits to the SAS have been reduced to 10, but for these men the toughest test is still to come – a three-day combat survival exercise in the Welsh mountains, under the watchful eye of Henno and Red Troop.

Dressed in World War II battledress – rough trousers without belts, greatcoats without buttons and boots without laces, they must navigate 100 miles across rough terrain. To help them, they are given a home-made silk map, two 10p pieces, matches and a compass. And to succeed, they must evade capture by 40 Paras acting the part of the enemy in the woods.

As the students file off the lorry and into the woods, they hear the roar of the Paras coming to ambush them even before their test has begun. One would-be trooper, Mick Sharp, rolls up his sleeve to reveal a Para tattoo and fares better than the others, particularly Luke, who has his ankle stamped on.

Henno blows a whistle and the soldiers are sent into the woods. Mick is put in a team with Louis Hoffman, Roger Trent and the injured Luke. They are given a grid reference for a rendezvous (RV) point the next day. If they miss it, they will have no food for another 24 hours. Over in another part of the woods, a man pulls up on a motorbike. He hides

it in the trees and, dressed in camouflage gear, sets off into the woods, carrying a knapsack.

Jamie and Mick are old friends, having met on selection before. It's Mick's last chance to pass selection as students are given two strikes then they're out. Henno is yet to be convinced. Jamie, however, has his own problems to sort out. Alex is behaving with increased animosity towards him but he can't work out why. He's unaware that Alex is interested in Caroline, while she, clearly, is only interested in Jamie.

Stumbling through the woods in the dead of night, Luke is separated from the others and is smashed in the face with a tree branch. His attacker is the mysterious man who arrived by motorbike, who tells him he'll never make the grade for SAS. As Mick, Trent and Louis come into sight of the RV point, Mick realizes Luke is missing. He and Trent go to

The would-be SAS recruits contemplate the task ahead.

Louis and Mick are swept away as they cross a raging river.

look for him, while Louis makes the RV point alone and guzzles his food so he doesn't have to share it.

Mick is late and tells Henno that Luke is missing, so Jamie and Jem are scrambled to find him. The students come up against a river and Mick's weakness is exposed – a fear of water. All three of them struggle to cross the fast current and are swept away.

Trent attempts to get a grip on the far bank when he is offered a hand up. His helper is the man who attacked Luke. Upstream, Louis and Mick haul themselves out and go in search of Trent. They find him dead.

Mick calls Henno from a phone box, but when Trent is airlifted away doctors discover he was murdered. The finger points at Mick, and Henno assembles Red Troop, even though police want the exercise called off.

Unaware of the new danger, Mick and Louis see only chaos at the next RV point and assume it is another ambush. Mick leaps up and runs straight at a man who is creeping up behind him, armed with a knife. Assuming he is a Para, Mick flees. In the midst of the chaos, the attacker produces a sawn-off shotgun. From the RV point, Henno hears two shots.

Against police orders, Red Troop go into the woods to hunt down the killer. But when they discover the truth about him, Henno's rage reaches boiling point. And the ordeal is still not over for Mick…

EPISODE 4 : BREAKOUT

Three armed Chechens break into a pharmaceutical plant which carries out tests for Foot and Mouth. Holding a professor at gunpoint, they obtain a phial

from a laboratory. A biochemist is shot, but not before she manages to sound the alarm and seal the unit. The thieves are trapped inside, along with three hostages.

Red Troop is summoned and Henno is instantly suspicious – why call the SAS to a break-in at a low-security organization? Smith of MI5 admits some anthrax spores have been released, and imposes a news blackout.

Box 500 hacks into the CCTV cameras and Red Troop see what they are up against. A woman lies still in a pool of blood and one of the Chechens is covered in grotesque blisters – apparently dead from exposure to the anthrax.

Faced with the evidence of the CCTV, Smith eventually admits to Colonel Dempsey that the company has been working on a vaccine for a form of anthrax. The mutation is a potent mix developed by the Russians and spliced with the flu virus. If the intruders were to release the microbes, thousands of people could die.

Henno and Dotsy put together a Deliberate Plan of Action, not knowing if the professor, Sergei Poliakoff, is innocent or working with the intruders. He appears to be dazed, while the lethal flask of anthrax is left vulnerable on a table nearby.

Smith speaks to the gang leader Ruslan who tells him that they will leave the anthrax and the hostages inside if they are given money. But Smith plays a double bluff. He tells Ruslan he will receive money while telling Henno that the Chechens are threatening to release the anthrax and the team must go in immediately. Then Ruslan and another

Above: *Henno slumps to the ground, bleeding profusely from a shotgun wound.*

Left: *Chechen terrorists Ruslan (left) and Moussa threaten to release a potent mix of anthrax if their demands are not met.*

Chechen, Moussa, realize that Sergei is ill, believing he is infected by the spores. Ruslan calls for a female doctor and Caroline volunteers.

Gathering the team, Dotsy explains the plan of attack. The Chechens are expected to follow Caroline on the CCTV cameras, leaving a blind spot through which Henno can move into position close by. Using Caroline as a decoy, he can take out the intruders and get the flask.

All appears to be going to plan until Caroline reaches the door, when Ruslan grabs the flask and rushes to the entrance, threatening to shoot her unless the soldier reveals himself. Henno has no choice but to throw down his weapons and go inside the building unarmed.

Inside the incident room there is confusion. How did Ruslan know Henno was there? They replay the CCTV tapes and Jamie notices Ruslan put his hand in his pocket. He must have been answering a hands-free mobile phone set. Someone had tipped him off. Suddenly there is a violent movement on the monitors as Moussa shoots Henno. His right arm is shattered and he slumps to the ground.

Something needs to be done fast. Dempsey takes control from Smith and tells the team to get ready for a full assault. Privately, however, he tells Dotsy to talk to Twamley, positioned in the basement. The only thing that can kill the bug is 1,000 degrees of heat. If Twamley blows the building, he will kill himself and the others – but he will do it if he has to.

Henno realizes Smith has lied to them and tries to calm the situation, but the psychotic Moussa becomes enraged and shoots him again, this time in the kidney. The team watch their leader fade via the CCTV cameras. Can they storm the building without being seen or is it down to Caroline to save the day?

EPISODE 5 : THE KILLING OF A ONE-EYED BOOKIE

Red Troop is sent to protect a would-be Unionist politician in Northern Ireland. Special Branch officer Steve Gelder has received information that there is going to be a hit on Bill Gracey and the SAS has to ensure it fails.

Jamie is given the job of impersonating Gracey, complete with a wig and moustache, and is staying with Gracey's wife and children in a small village in South Armagh, guarded covertly by the rest of the team. As Jamie says goodbye to his 'family', Alex notices a scout watching but he is unarmed and sneaks off. Jamie is given the all clear to drive off, with Henno and Caroline following a short distance behind.

They unexpectedly hit a police roadblock and Henno knows instantly that something is wrong. The policemen are not in the right uniform. At the same time, one of the terrorists, Maguire, sees Henno is carrying a pistol. As Jamie simultaneously reaches for his gun, the younger 'officer' Sean hits him with the butt of his own pistol. Gunfire breaks out and under a siege of bullets one of the men, Kieran, is shot, while Jamie is bundled into the getaway car. Suddenly, the driver Sweeney realises with horror that Gracey is not Gracey at all. They have the wrong man, but it is too late to dump him. The throat mike reveals he

Henno is furious when Jamie is kidnapped by terrorists in Northern Ireland.

is a valuable hostage – they need him as security.

Henno is furious, though his anger may be more a disguise for his genuine upset at losing a man, while Dotsy tries hard to push the official line of congratulations for a successful mission. But for the troopers it's not a good result. Jamie is somewhere in the Republic – dead or alive – and they have no way of reaching him.

Irish MI5 operative Vanessa Kennington allows the team access to some classified information on Gracey and the man who warned them about the hit – Jack Cullen, an undercover operative now working as a double agent high within the ranks of the IRA. Rumour has it that they murdered a bookie.

Alex recognizes the picture of Cullen as the scout and Henno questions the loyalties of someone who has been working undercover for seven years. Whoever he is really working for, however, he is sure to know where Jamie is being kept. As Henno and Caroline break orders and head off into the Republic, Twamley goes off with Jem, determined to prove that they all share the responsibility for Jamie's loss. At a housing estate in Armagh, Twamley looks up an old flame called Mary, whose brother may have information.

When Republican intelligence officer Matt Shaunessy returns to his house a few hours later, Jem and Twamley jump him and demand to know where the safe house is. But Shaunessy does not return alone – he is accompanied by Gracey's daughter Georgia. Unbeknown to her, Shaunessy has been using Georgia for information about her father.

At the safe house, Jamie is being battered by interrogation, both mentally and physically. He's resilient, even under the torture of a burning poker. Then Maguire takes him outside and forces him into a grave. As Maguire raises his gun, Jamie finally breaks.

As the members of Red Troop put their careers on the line to find Cullen and the safe house, they know that they may already be too late…

EPISODE 6 : SOMETHING TO DO WITH JUSTICE

The operation to save Jamie in Ireland has cost Henno his career. He and Pete Twamley have been kicked out of Red Troop for their unauthorized excursions into the Republic. Forced to hand in all their gear, they leave the regiment. Unable to work in an official capacity, Henno finds a job where their training can be put to good use unofficially. In the office of ex-SAS member Steven Flint, Henno and Twamley are offered a 'very nice little earner'.

Much to Jem Poynton's disgust, Johnny Bell is made leader of Red Troop and the team prepares for their next mission – to a classified destination. But Jamie cannot accept things so easily and goes to visit Henno at home. Henno's brusque behaviour does nothing to make this irregular visit any easier and Jamie feels leaving just as awkward as when he arrived.

Red Troop, joined by new recruit Mick Sharp, is finally told where they are going – Bosnia. Caroline briefs the team at an SFOR base. She shows them a photo of the target, Glasnovic, a Bosnian Serb wanted in the Hague for war crimes. But 'lifting' him is no easy task.

Red Troop begin surveillance and in the early hours of the morning, Jamie and Mick spot a car arriving at the encampment. Through his scope, Jamie recognizes the forms of Henno and Twamley. He's shocked but also amused – what is going on? Henno and Twamley are welcomed by Boban Haradic and the beautiful Masha. But they are not trusted, and Henno is forced to undergo a full body examination.

Back at the SFOR barn, Jem Poynton is furious. Caroline and Dotsy explain that MI5 had got wind of Glasnovic approaching Flint's private security firm wanting ex-SAS personnel to train his militia in close protection and weapons. The timing was perfect – the CO (commanding officer) needed to be seen to be punishing Twamley and Henno, while the Serbs would believe they were genuinely not operational. Dotsy also reveals that Haradic is thought to be behind the massacre of a village.

Henno and Twamley meanwhile meet three men identically dressed as Glasnovic and realize why he has proved to be such a difficult target. Talking loudly next to the camouflaged hide of Jamie and Ricky Mann, Haradic says he got the idea from Saddam Hussein. This is not good news. Dotsy can't risk authorising the killing of a civilian. He may be forced to scrap the operation – but how will they get Henno and Twamley out?

Henno also finds himself drawn to Masha. They sleep together and she unwittingly gives him the vital piece of information that can put Red Troop

Masha shows whose side she's really on in Bosnia.

Jamie holds Glasnovic/Haradic at gunpoint at the showdown in the Bosnian compound.

back on target. Swedish journalists are coming to interview Glasnovic. Henno writes a plan of attack, which Twamley hides in a tree.

When the journalists arrive, Major Robin of SFOR confiscates their passports and gives them to Caroline. She will have to be the woman, and, despite Jem's protestation that he is right for the job, Jamie fits the photograph. As Ricky gives them intensive language coaching, Alex and Mick fit the TV camera with a location transmitter.

Henno and Twamley are in the armoury when the 'television crew' arrive. Henno searches Caroline so the Serbs don't realise that she is concealing a firearm. Then Henno and Twamley lead the militia men off for a firing practice while Jamie presses the record button on his camera, sending a signal to Dotsy that the target is on site. But when Red Troop close in on the compound, all guns blazing, things do not go entirely to plan. One member of the team is left fighting for life…

MAIN CAST

MAIN CAST

Henno Garvie	Ross Kemp
Jamie Dow	Jamie Draven
Alex Leonard	Sendhil Ramamurthy
Pete Twamley	Tony Curran
Ricky Mann	Danny Sapani
Jem Poynton	Elliot Cowan
Captain Caroline Walshe	Alex Reid
Lt Dotsy Doheny	Jamie Bamber
Colonel Aidan Dempsey	Miles Anderson
Johnny Bell	Chris Ryan
Box 500	Tobias Menzies
Sam Leonard	Anthony Howell
Mick Sharp	Laurence Fox
Mrs Twamley	Jackie Morrison
Brian Duggan	Tom Georgeson
Badger	Eddie Marsan
Weasel	Russell Tovey
Lofty	Francis Magee
Pug	Robert Willox
Bill Jackson	Peter Wight
Stuart	Sam Troughton
Simon	Jamie Sives
Lorraine	Madeleine Worrall
Mrs Leonard	Carmen Du Sautoy
Flossie	Inday Ba
Rod	Barney Craig
Louis Hoffman	Christopher Fox
Billy Dwyer	Alex Palmer
Roger Trent	Josh Cole
DI Wallace	Paul Brennen
Moussa	Serge Soric

Ruslan .... Dragan Micanovic
Eli .... Goran Kostic
Smith .... Nick Dunning
Sergei Poliakoff .... Rad Lazar
Griffin .... Jonathan Coy
Jack Cullen .... Dermot Crowley
Sean Weir .... Damian O'Hare
Fintan Maguire .... David Wilmot
Steve Gelder .... Colum Convey
Vanessa Kennington .... Cara Kelly
Mary .... Clare Cathcart
Boban Haradic .... Velibor Topic
Masha .... Ana Sofrenovic
Dude .... Mirko Sekulic
Savo Glasnovic .... Andreas Wisniewski
Major Robin .... Lawrence Ellman

PRODUCTION CREDITS

Executive Producer .... Brian True-May
Producer .... Peter Norris
Director (Episodes 1–2) .... Diarmuid Lawrence
Director (Episodes 3–4) .... Tom Clegg
Director (Episodes 5–6) .... Tim Leandro
Creators .... Rob Heyland
                                                                                      Chris Ryan
Writers .... Rob Heyland
                                                                                      Len Collin
                                                                                      Julian Jones
Consultant .... Chris Ryan
Director of Photography .... Kevin Rowley
Line Producer .... Ian Strachan

Production Designer	Gary Williamson
Location Manager	Rupert Bray
Casting	Jane Arnell
Costume Designer	Reg Samuel
Make-up Designer	Vanessa Johnson
Sound Recordist	Richard Reynolds
Script Editor	Emma Kingsman-Lloyd
1st Assistant Directors	Max Keene
	Dominic Fysh
Special Effects Co-ordinator	Tony Harding
Stunt Co-ordinator	Colin Skeaping
Editors	Ardan Fisher
	Derek Bain
Music	Rick Wentworth

SAS
SPEAK

SAS SPEAK

Bergen A large rucksack, carried by British forces on active service, containing a basic survival kit of food, water, shelter, sleeping bag and clothes. During selection, SAS students are asked to carry Bergens weighing 50lb or more.

Big Four Number, rank, name, date of birth. The only four pieces of information which an enemy is allowed to ask for under the terms of the Geneva Convention.

Box 500 The Post Office address of MI5, which in *Ultimate Force* is the name of a character from intelligence.

COBRA Cabinet-level approval for an operation, usually involving the Prime Minister.

CRW Counter Revolutionary Warfare. The division of the SAS to which Red Troop belong.

Deniable Anything agreed by word rather than in writing is deniable and breaks the line of responsibility. Used by the SAS, other military departments and the Government.

Dicker A look-out, usually used for the enemy. A friendly look-out is a 'stag'.

DPA Deliberate Plan of Action. A considered way in which the operation will proceed. Usually gets overtaken by IPA – Immediate Plan of Action by which the SAS go in all guns blazing.

DPMs Clothing made from destructive pattern material used for camouflage.

Escape and Evasion An exercise where soldiers have to move from one rendezvous point to another while avoiding attack by members of a regiment acting the part of a hunter force.

Explosive Entry Unlike armed police SO19, part of SAS procedure includes blowing their way into a building.

FMP Forward Mounting Position from where an attack is launched.

Harvey wallbanger A cannon that can blow a hole in a brick wall.

Len Dickson A belt containing holsters for guns.

Man down When one of the troop is struck down or killed in an operation, another member must give this information to the command centre, using the throat microphone, and continue. Stopping to offer assistance could cost another life.

Necessary Force When the SAS are called in, there is a military rather than a peaceful solution. Necessary force frequently means 'kill everything that moves'.

CO Officer commanding the squadron.

OP Observation post. Building a good OP is an important part of the SAS's ability to get in and out of a position without being seen or detected.

RTU Returned to Unit. If a soldier is sacked from the SAS or fails selection, he may be sent back to his original regiment, amid great loss of pride.

Rupert A nickname used by soldiers for an officer. Not always derogatory.

RV Rendezvous point used on exercise. ERV is an Emergency Rendezvous.

Tap, tap Special Forces often use the technique of firing two precision shots in quick succession, rather than random automatic firing, meaning to get down and stay down. Henno trains Jamie to 'double tap' through the mouth so there is no chance of a signal getting into the enemy's hand to fire.

Thermic lance A lightweight system designed for cutting through steel during an assault on a building.

TQ Tactical questioning. Part of selection where would-be troopers are questioned, ridiculed, sometimes forced to strip and humiliated in a bid to get them to reveal classified information.

VCP Vehicle checkpoint.

Vindaloos Fireproof underwear, part of the kit given to an SAS trooper.

X-Ray A target in an operation. X-Rays are numbered and reported back by number to the command centre as they are dealt with.

Yankee A hostage. Each hostage is given a number for ease of reference during an operation.

INDEX